What is a Ghost?

By Richard Felix

FELIX FILMS

To Guy

What is a Ghost?

Happy Haunting

First published in Great Britain in 2009 by
Felix Films Ltd
Derbyshire

Distributed by Felix Films Ltd, The Studios, Derbyshire , DE6 5JJ
Tel: 0845 88 22 782
Www.felixfilms.net

ISBN 978-0-9557535-3-4

Printed in Ireland by ColourBooks

CONTENTS

This book is dedicated to the three most precious people in my life, Julia, Edd and Wills.

ACKNOWLEDGEMENTS

The production of this book would never have been possible without the knowledge and expertise of:

Julia Felix
William Felix
Edward Felix
Harriet Woodward
Daniel Mason
C. J. Romer
Wayne Anthony
Steve Lilley
David Hurn
Chris Fleming
Patrick Burns
Jacky Newcomb
Jason Hawes
Steve Parsons
Derek Acorah
Dr Matthew Smith
Stacey Jones
Chris / Eleanor Thompson
Tarka King
Sammie Leslie
Sir Humphrey Wakefield
Jeff Belanger
Paul / Sue James

FOREWORD

I was delighted when I learned that Richard Felix was about to publish a book about his theories on ghosts and more than honoured when he asked whether I would add a word or two in the form of this foreword.

I first met Richard some six years ago during the filming of a paranormal programme upon which we were both working. The place was Derby Gaol. Upon meeting him, I was immediately taken by Richard's incredible enthusiasm as he related the history of the location and his obvious love of his home town of Derby.

As I was to find out over the ensuing years, Richard's knowledge of the history of our country and beyond is boundless. His manner of delivering the facts is riveting. I have spent many hours with Richard during paranormal investigations in some very strange and dark places waiting for 'something to happen'. During those times he has fascinated me with some of his stories of days gone by. I am sure that within the pages of this, Richard's latest book, you will be equally enthralled.

I can think of no one better to share his theories on ghosts and the Paranormal than Richard, Ghost Historian Extraordinaire!

DEREK ACORAH

PREFACE

In 1992 Richard Felix decided that his home town of Derby desperately needed a Heritage Centre as a catalyst for him to tell the history of his city, not only to its residents but also to the whole world. Little did he realise what a far-reaching effect the opening of this centre would have and that it would lead to the origins of the now world famous Derby Ghost Walks, that have attracted people from all over the world, which has now established Derby as 'The Ghost Capital of Great Britain.'

The walks not only tell the ghost stories of the city but also delve into the fascinating history behind them. Richard is a great believer that ghosts and history go together.

The ghost walks have evolved over the last fourteen years and now offer the public two different experiences. The City Centre Ghost Walk, starting from The Old Bell in Sadlergate, tells the infamous story of PC Moss, the only police officer in Derbyshire to be murdered in the line of duty. After hearing this story it is time for a well earned drink in The Old Tiger Inn before descending into the Guildhall Tunnels - where you might get the fright of your life. The walk continues around the city centre visiting various haunted sites including The Jorrocks Pub, final resting place of a screaming skull. The tour finishes back at the Old Bell with a visit to the attic room haunted by the ghost of a serving maid. The evening concludes with a candle-lit supper in the Old Tudor Bar.

With the success of The City Centre Ghost Walk, Richard discovered another building which was to add to the ghostly stories and tell the tales of crime and punishment in Derby. This was the Derby Gaol, located in the basement of 50/51 Friar Gate. This building was erected in 1756 and was the second of three county gaols in Derby. It remained a place of incarceration and execution until 1840. Richard set about restoring it to its original structure with his usual enthusiasm and expertise.

During the renovation the original graffiti was

discovered on the cell doors. These were the carvings of prisoners scratching their initials on them the day before they were hanged. The public are now able to visit the gaol and wander around the cells seeing the condemned cell and the etchings for themselves. The Hangsman Walk was born starting from the Derby Gaol telling the stories of murders, executions and ghostly occurrences. The visitor starts with a brief tour of the Gaol before heading down Agard Street, to hear of the harrowing murder of Eliza Morrow in 1862. Continuing down Friar Gate for the first haunted pub stop, Seymours, there is a picture of the Victorian lady who haunts the pub to this day. The walk continues into the cellars of the Old Friary before returning to the Gaol for supper and then unlike so many others, the visitor will be allowed to return home after making sure that no one follows them.

The fame of these walks and Derby Gaol spread worldwide and as a result Richard came to the notice of the hugely popular Living TV programme 'Most Haunted.' The team came along and carried out interviews, paranormal investigations with the latest hi-tech ghost hunting equipment. On returning to the editing studios they could not decide which part of Richard's interview to edit - as a result Richard was appointed as the resident paranormal historian on the programme - and the rest is most haunted history!

Derby Gaol has now become a major tourist attraction and one of the 'must do' haunted locations in this country. Offering not only ghost walks but night vigils, using the latest equipment and offering the services of a spiritualist medium.

Richard realised how the public are excited about ghost hunting and the history connected to buildings and with his friend Stephen Lilley they set about the enormous and time-consuming task of creating the Ghost Tour Of Great Britain. They produced a series of books and DVD's called 'The Ghost Tour Of Great Britain.' They have now visited over 40 counties throughout England, Scotland and Wales. In September 2005 Richard's youngest son William set up his own production company called 'Felix Films Ltd' which will endeavour to complete Richard's tour of Haunted Britain.`

The ghost tour team, left to right Steve Lilley, Delicia Redfern and Richard Felix.

WHAT THE EXPERTS THINK...

DR MATTHEW SMITH, Associate Professor in Psychology, Liverpool Hope University.

Anybody who says they know what a ghost is, are lying. People may have opinions as to what they think a ghost is, but nobody really knows for sure. Many apparent experiences of ghosts can, in my opinion, be explained in terms of beliefs and expectations influencing the way people interpret fairly mundane phenomena like knocks and bangs, changes in temperature, tricks of the light and so on. The really impressive, and less easy to explain cases are when several people report seeing recognizable apparitions of people who have recently died. But the question remains whether they are spirits of the dead.

DEREK ACORAH 'Medium'

As a Spirit Medium I do not generally tend to talk about ghosts but prefer to refer to the higher side of life as spirit people. In my work as a Medium during my theatre demonstrations I am constantly in communication with these returned spirits, either directly or through my spirit guide Sam. They are as real to me as anybody who happens to be living in physical form on the earth today.

However the side of my work which involves investigative mediumship, I do then come into contact with phenomena which could be termed as ghosts. These are the shadowy figures who lurk in old houses, castles, broken ruins or maybe can be seen drifting across a road on a dark night. They can appear as wisps of ethereal mist or they can appear almost in solid form. They are not the returned spirits of people who have lived or worked in a building or area, but are more a memory of those people - a photograph in time if you like.

Whilst living, the energy of a person or people who have resided in a building is absorbed into the fabric of the location. Long after physical death, that energy remains. This is why it is possible for the ghost of a well known person, Mary Queen of Scots for instance, to be observed in a number of different locations at the same time… even simultaneously. The phenomena that people are viewing is merely a memory- the residual energy of times gone by. It is not the spirit of Mary Queen of Scots but merely the ghost of that lady.

The more emotional or tragic the events which have taken place in a property, the stronger the energies that are absorbed and so, the greater the opportunity of glimpsing a ghost. The stronger the personality of a person who has lived in a building, then the more likely it is that the person's energies will be greater in a property than a more weak and ineffectual personality.

There are many types of ghost; there are anniversary ghosts and crisis ghosts. There are headless ghosts and legless ghosts, but these are merely memories from the past. The spirit return of Anne Boleyn, for instance, would not see that lady popping up with her head under her arm as is popularly perceived. What people have viewed is a ghost… either that or they have a very fertile imagination!

So to me, a ghost is a memory whilst a spirit is a person, as real now as they ever were in their physical life.

STACEY JONES 'Ghost Cop'

A ghost is an imprint of energy from a person or personality (or sometimes even an animal) who has passed on. They can manifest themselves in many ways and reports of ghosts have transcended all cultures, religion.

Ghosts may be caught between dimensions or plains and be here with us because they may not know they have passed on, have unfinished business, are afraid to cross over or just prefer to be here with their loved ones.

CHRIS FLEMING 'Dead Famous'

A fully manifested ghost is a visual form that acts as a representation of the life the soul last had. A ghost represents either how his or her spirit (soul) wants to be remembered or how we would remember it when they were alive in their physical form. Because one sees a ghost it does not necessarily mean the spirit of the actual person is present. Souls that have crossed over to the spirit plane, can in some instances send a part of them back. This part which becomes an image is a ghost of their former self. This image is not their true form they take while in the spirit world. You could consider this type of ghost in some cases a projected moving photo or video that they want us to see. In other sightings a ghost can also represent an actual person, not just an image.

Spirits that are earthbound and have not crossed over have not rejoined with their true higher self so therefore are not aware of who they truly are and where they have originally come from. They tend to be lost. When they appear in our physical realm (third dimension) and we see them either by chance or if they allow themselves to be seen, their ghostly appearance is how they last remember themselves when they were alive. Their ghostly image can appear in various stages until they fully manifest into a complete image of their last life form. Whether as a soldier, a nurse, a mailman, or whatever they felt they were most known for or felt most comfortable with in their last lifetime.

People that have been murdered or suffered violent deaths may still be trapped in the emotional trauma and will tend to appear in the death image and be viewed how they looked during their last moments of death. This ghostly image can be startling and shocking not only to the ghost itself, but the viewer who happens to see them.

Overall, a fully manifested ghost represents a complete visual form that can be identified by gender and appearance. The details seen during a complete manifestation help us see who they once were. This image we have come accustomed to calling 'a ghost.'

When it comes to partial manifestations and glimpses of the flowing conscious energy that we all have and are a part of, the images and visuals can vary. After death our soul (spirit) is outside the body and no longer applies to the 3rd dimensional physics we had been originally accustomed to. We find that our spirit and conscious energy (mind) no longer has use for arms, legs, etc. The new world we are moving into has interaction by pure thought and not by physical responses we were originally accustomed to. If we want to interact back in the third dimension it takes our mind and consciousness to alter and affect the existing energy in the 3rd dimension before it can interact with 3rd dimensional forms. We cannot just jump right in and start touching or moving things, we first must affect the air (ions) and existing energy around us in that physical environment we step into. If we choose to appear in the physical world and are seen either by mistake or intent the stages we are thinking ourselves into to create our form, can be begin and/or be seen in any stage from a ball of light, to a dark mist or light mist as well as glow or streak or energy. At times these forms can be mistaken for ghosts, but without no true form it is hard to tell what we are looking at let alone what gender or what the person may look like. Once we fully manifest into what we remember ourselves to look like all prior stages up to that point cannot be considered a true 'ghost!' Shadow forms and fully manifested shadow forms with arms, legs head etc. can be considered ghosts, yet they have not chosen to enlighten us with their full facial features or details to what they are wearing or look like. Their dark form represents, I want you to see me as I am here, but not all of me. There are many reasons for this, secrecy, fear, shyness and in some cases intimidation.

What we must understand, when we die, we can all appear as a ghost, if and only if we fully choose to and learn how to. For some it will be frustrating for others it will be a new way of life, but to us still in the physical it continues to remain strange and partially unknown 'phenomenon.'

PATRICK BURNS 'Haunting Evidence'

I believe a ghost is best defined as… "the scientifically intangible essence of energy that exists after the human body has expired or died." We know that in physics, the law of conservation states that energy is neither created nor destroyed, but merely transformed from one form into another. If this law is universally constant or true, **something** by definition must survive physical death. The question for the scholars is, does this energy retain its intellect, knowledge and memories it had as a living being? The illusive nature of this energy is what I mean by "scientifically intangible" - if one cannot replicate their evidence of the existence of ghosts under controlled observations, then ghosts cannot be scientifically substantiated. So they remain a mystery.

JACKY NEWCOMB

'The Angel Lady'

Ghosts: I think many people get confused between ghosts and spirits - or perhaps it is just down to interpretation? Ghosts are 'energy memory', sometimes a recording on the atmosphere of a past real life experience (baby crying, army marching etc).

Buildings and many other objects can record 'life energy' in the way that magnetic tape records the voice, and certain conditions (water, electrical storms and so on) can help to release that recording into the atmosphere which enables us to see a 'ghost' of an experience that happened in earlier times.

Memories of high passion (love or hate) make the strongest 'recordings' so if you are unlucky enough to be staying in an old house with a moat during a thunder storm its quite possible that the 'ghost' (energy memory) of a traumatic time (i.e. someone was stabbed to death), will re-play in front of you at the bottom of your hotel bedroom! Scary! But it is just a 'memory' and although you might see… and indeed experience the feelings of that time being re-played in front of you the vision will not harm you in any way.

Spirits: I believe that anything else is spirit, or souls with intelligence and awareness. Spirits who are either 'trapped' in our atmosphere due to traumatic death experiences or unfinished business (they might not even realise they are dead) or spirits visiting locations on the earth plane for their own reasons.

Spirits might be aware of our existence, they might see us, or have no knowledge that we are sharing the same 'space' as them (they might not see us at all).

Of course there is a third option - a ghost could be a

figment of our imagination - a shadow or similar! But in my personal experience a 'ghost' in your own home is usually a relative popping in to say "HELLO"!

STEVE PARSONS 'Para.Science'

What is a Ghost is the eternal question that all of us engaged in Psychical Research have been striving to be able to answer. It could be argued that science really only took a serious interest in trying to answer the question in 1882 following the formation of the Society for Psychical Research before then the question either wasn't asked as society simply accepted Ghosts and Spirits as part of their (unseen) world or was occasionally tackled by philosophers and men of religion.

There are many who already claim to know what Ghosts are; Spiritualists inform us that they are the trapped souls of the deceased unable or unwilling to move on to the higher planes of existence. Parapsychologists may offer the opinion that Ghosts represent nothing more than hallucinations or some other unkind trick of the mind. There are countless paranormal investigation teams, throughout the USA and Britain; many with their own theories and notions about the nature of Ghosts and how they manifest.

In the modern hunt for an answer many different methods are employed: Good old fashioned séances still prevail. Ouija boards and dowsing rods remain popular tools of the ghost hunter. Modern technology has allowed us to peer into the darkest cellar and spookiest hiding place of Ghosts using Infra Red and Thermal Imaging. The Electromagnetic spectrum is scanned for the energy used or manipulated by Ghosts and Spirits by a variety of EMF meters and the voices of the dead are listened for using modified radios and computer software. All so far (sadly) to no avail. Despite the claims by many, we still lack that most crucial item of equipment for the Ghost Hunter – The Ghost Detector! But, then that is hardly surprising when one considers that if we cannot detect or measure something how do we know if ghosts exist at all.

It is a truth perhaps not universally acclaimed that at the end of the first decade of the 21st Century we still do not have an answer to the question 'What is a Ghost.'

JASON HAWES

TAPS 'Ghost Hunters'

I believe there are multiple types of Ghosts, one being the inner energy of ourselves after we pass. It still has knowledge and understanding and decides to stay for whatever reason it may have. Also I believe there is a style of what we call a Ghost which is not a Ghost at all, sometimes we catch voices and sounds that are saying things as if normal every day life is still going on for them. As if they can not hear us. This type of a 'Ghost' I believe to be nothing but a slit somewhere in time. As if all times are somehow connected.

DARREN STANTON 'psychological coach and mind magician'

Definitively a ghost - or spirit or apparition - is the energy, soul or personality of a person who has died and has somehow got stuck between this plane of existence and the next. Most researchers believe that these spirits do not know they are dead. Very often they have died under traumatic, unusual or highly emotional circumstances. Ghosts can be perceived by the living in a number of ways: through sight (apparitions), sound (voices), smell (fragrances and odours), touch - and sometimes they can just be sensed. After conducting paranormal investigations all over the UK for the past ten years, I believe that 99.9 % of experiences that people have can be explained by either psychological or scientific means but for me the most intriguing evidence lies within the 1%. of the equation. Although I can replicate a lot of paranormal phenomena through magic, suggestion and psychology, I have many experiences which allow that door of perception within my mind to remain ajar. Our ability to have an experience or not is largely attributable to someone's belief system. We as humans will always produce the evidence to support the belief. If someone does not even consider the possibility that something may exist then even if a full apparition presented itself in front of the absolute sceptic the chances are they probably would not even see it.

JEFF BELANGER Founder of Ghostvillage.com, author of 'The World's Most Haunted Places', and host of '30 Odd Minutes'.

It is a big question with profound implications. A ghost is a direct link to our past, an emotional connection with everyone around us in our present, and a glimpse of our own inevitable future. A ghost is history demanding to be remembered, or at the very least acknowledged. A ghost enables us to safely discuss death, a subject that makes most of us squirm under normal circumstances. And sometimes a ghost is just a coincidence. What a ghost is very much depends on the perceptions of the witness. We all have our baggage: our level of education, our religious beliefs, our socioeconomic status, and what our parents told us was real and not real. We cannot escape who we are. Four different people could witness an identical phenomenon and reach four different conclusions. For example, an atheist, a ghost hunter, a Baptist, and a science fiction fan walk into a bar (sounds like a good setup to a joke, no?) and see a misty figure form into the shape of a woman dressed in eighteenth-century dress and float through the far wall. The atheist believes he is over-tired, perhaps he had too much to drink, and now he has seen a hallucination. The ghost hunter leaps with excitement and proclaims this is a ghost and must be some kind of residual energy leftover from the past that has just replayed and after all, this is a bar, there are bound to have been some deaths. The Baptist falls to his knees praying to his Creator. He believes this figure to be a demon sent by God to punish him for entering a locale as nefarious as a bar. The science fiction fan believes he just saw a glitch in the matrix. What do these four people have in common besides witnessing the same thing? They all believe to their core that their conclusion is the only correct one Religiously speaking, ghosts are the least common denominator of spirituality. Jews see ghosts, as do Christians, Muslims, Buddhists, Hindus, and even atheists. There's a big question floating around all of us. It gnaws at us late at night like a hunger that must eventually be satisfied. What happens to us after we die? If you experience what you believe to be a ghost or a spirit, that big question is answered for you. *Something* happens after we die. We do go on. What spiritual path you take beyond that will vary, but the implication of the encounter is huge.

Scientifically speaking, there may also be answers as to what a ghost is. Quantum psychics comes along and suggests time isn't necessarily linear. *That* would explain many a ghost sighting, wouldn't it? You didn't just see a group of ghost soldiers marching across that battlefield, you saw a flicker of the past, just for a brief moment for a reason we don't fully understand just yet. Another quantum theory poses that there may be an infinite number of dimensions, or parallel universes, if you will, and perhaps those dimensions bump into each other. We see them, perhaps they see us, and then it is over. A ghost. Boo!

Some people want to see a ghost so badly that every fluttering curtain is a sign from the other side. Others are delusional, or on drugs, and hallucinating something they believe to be real. And then there is fraud: ghosts have become big business. Many restaurants, pubs, inns, and other businesses are eager to exploit their haunted reputations for monetary gain. Some even go so far as to rig contraptions that might offer an artificial ghost experience to its patrons.

RON KOLEK 'New England Ghost Project', Presenter of 'Ghost Chronicles'

Maureen Wood, my partner and fifth generation psychic despises the word 'ghost'. She prefers 'spirit'. Maybe it's the negative connotation associated with it through its use in books, stories and movies, but as for me, being politically correct is not so important. I prefer ghost. I define the word ghost as any spectral entity either living or dead. You might laugh at the thought of a living spectral entity, but actually it is quite obvious. Living is loosely defined as having life or existence.

It is widely accepted within the paranormal community that there are generally two types of haunting: residual and intelligent. A residual haunting or 'ghost' is nothing more than an imprint in the time and fabric of our universe without the ability to interact, hence 'dead'. Whereas an intelligent haunting or "ghost", possesses not only the ability to interact with its environment, but also under certain circumstances, even understand it. They possess both intelligence and personality, hence "living". So what separates the ghost from other spectral entities? It is simple; the ghost once had a body. To me, it is these traits that characterize the word ghost

SIR HUMPHREY WAKEFIELD, owner of Chillingham Castle.

Some ghosts are the happy few who do not want to move on. I know that end of party feeling so well and so hope to join them in my time. Other ghosts are angry. They need to solve their problems and revenges before moving on, and I understand that too. Other ghosts, again, have good works to complete and stay on to urge and direct the living. I feel that lot almost too strongly. Ghosts are always there, but they are most noticeable when other factors do not blind out their subtle strengths.

EDD FELIX, Derby ghost walks.

Although I have been taking ghost walks around Derby for five years, I am still a sceptic. I have spoken to thousands of rational people who have no reason to make up stupid stories. Therefore I believe them. A ghost is in my opinion someone who has unfinished business on this earth and has not moved on.

INTRODUCTION

"Do you believe in ghosts"? said she
"and from whence do such things stem."
"No I replied, I don't believe.
But I'm still afraid of them."
Anon.

For the last fifty six years I have been haunted by ghosts but I do not see dead people, I am not a medium, I do not sense things I do not feel things, in fact I am a psychic brick. Take me into any alleged haunted building and I will feel nothing apart from fear. I am frightened of ghosts and have been since the age of four. No not just frightened but terrified. As a small child I played with children who were a lot older and they would lock me in a garage and tell me stories about a 'green ghost' that would be waiting to 'get me' when I went home to bed. I obviously had a very vivid imagination at this age, like so many young children. As a result of this my mother would have to spend hours sitting by my bed waiting for me to go to sleep. Very often she would have to leave me still awake on my own after sitting with me for many hours. When she left my bedroom I would become so frightened waiting for the green ghost to come and 'get me'. Every night I had the same bedtime ritual once I was left alone in my room. First I would implore my mother to leave the door open and the landing light turned on. Then I would keep calling down to her so that I still had communication with someone. However, the time always came when I was all alone. I would hide under the bed covers holding down the covers with my head in case it would try and pull them off. Next I would cross my fingers, count up to sixty and then feign deep sleep. This I did in the vain hope that anything ghostly lingering in my room would think that I was fast asleep and would leave me alone. This was the way I went to sleep, summer and winter every night for most of my childhood years. I think I was at least fourteen before I would even venture upstairs on my own to the toilet. Nothing ever happened to me thank goodness, until the age of twenty seven which you will read about later in this book.

This type of fear lingers with you for the whole of your life in the same way that folk are frightened of moths, snakes, rats... the fear never goes away. No matter how many haunted places I visit it does not make it any easier and I will always try and not be left alone if there is any way of avoiding this situation. So why do I keep subjecting myself to this?... I do not know, perhaps it is a form of therapy. However, I have come to the conclusion that we all have a purpose in life and mine is to try and prove beyond all doubt that there are such things as ghosts and that the dead do return!

I do genuinely believe that ghosts exist as I have seen a ghost, heard a ghost and travelled with a ghost, but if you dance on the M6 long enough you will eventually be hit by a car. The same thing applies to folk who continually visit haunted locations. However, I still remain a sceptic, as I believe that eight out of ten ghostly occurrences can be explained... it was the wind that blew the door shut, someone had left the window open and it was a windy night. The dark shadow leaving your bedroom at 5 o'clock in the morning was in fact your dad. He was on an early shift and he had run out of socks and come into your room to raid your sock drawer. The ghostly apparition in the factory was actually Fred who was late clocking off from the previous shift. You just did not know that he was still in the building.

Most of my young working life was devoted to the sale of pop records in Derby Market Hall and apart from sales of singles such as 'There is a Ghost in My House', 'Monster Mash' and 'Ghost Busters' I did not come in contact with the paranormal. My destiny, without me realising, started to go in a very different direction when in 1992 I opened Derby Heritage Centre. The building had been an old Tudor grammar school dating back to 1554. It was built on the site of a graveyard and plague pit. Most of Derby's famous boys such as John Flamstead, The First Astronomer Royal, Reverend

Derby Heritage Centre.

Reverend John Cotton.

John Cotton Pilgrim Father and founder of Boston Massachusetts, and Joseph Wright were all educated at the school. Two Catholic priests, one of which was Nicholas Garlic, who was educated at the school, were found hiding in 1588 in a priest hole, in Padley Hall. They were brought back to Derby to be hanged, drawn and quartered for their faith. Due to the connection of Nicholas with the school I had a replica priest hole dug under the floor in Derby Heritage Centre. Whilst the builders were excavating they discovered three skeletons which caused all manner of paranormal and ghostly activity in the building to start. One of these ghostly apparitions was that of a young boy, about twelve years of age, who was seen on frequent occasions in the dormitories upstairs. After this I was always afraid of being in the building on my own. This created a tremendous interest with our customers and I realised how much interest and unanswered questions we all have about ghosts and the paranormal. As a result I realised that there was a business opportunity in creating ghost walks around my beloved city. As a result in 1993 the Derby Ghost Walk was 'born' and so was my involvement with everything paranormal. Three years later I opened Derby Gaol which was also very haunted and atmospheric. The ghost walk that evolved was unique and is still changing today as we add more and more paranormal stories and ghostly sightings that we gather from just talking with the general public. The ghost walk is an evening's entertainment consisting of three hours, two haunted pubs and a candle lit supper at the end. During the evening there is plenty of opportunity for the ghost hunters to talk to one another without the worry of being ridiculed, as they are in the company of like minded and interested people. The paranormal and ghostly experiences that folk tell me about frequently have many similarities and you soon realise that most people are telling the truth and not making things up. They have nothing to gain only peace of mind and very often they go home feeling better knowing that other folk have had similar experiences and that there is really no need to be afraid.

Richard Felix after a York ghost walk in the Golden Fleece Pub.

Sixteen years ago I could sit in a pub and ask a group of ghost walkers “has anyone seen a ghost?” If I was lucky three people would put up their hand and then they would possibly be ridiculed by the others on the ghost walk. Now its a very different kettle of fish. At least ten hands will go up and there will be no ridiculing. This does not mean that more people are seeing ghosts, it just means that more people are not frightened to talk about their ghostly experiences.

For the last sixteen years I have been conducting ghost tours around my home city of Derby and for the past nine years I have been visiting haunted places whilst completing a series of DVD’s titled ‘The National Ghost Tour of Great Britain.’ During my travels I have visited over six hundred haunted locations in England, Scotland, Wales, and Northern Ireland. Six years ago I became the historian on the TV programme Most Haunted and appeared on one hundred and twenty two episodes. During my ghost hunting career I must have visited well over one thousand allegedly haunted locations and have experienced many events that I cannot explain.

I would like to take this opportunity to thank Karl Beaty and Yvette Fielding for the experience of working on Most Haunted. Ghosts are my profession and they have helped my profile immensely. The programme has also created an amazing awareness in all things paranormal and has created more argument, more debate, more discussion, and more research than any other ghost programme.

With the success of the Derby Ghost Walks and the interest they have created Derby was voted the Most Haunted City in Great Britain, and Derby Gaol won an award for the best paranormal location in the British Isles. Derby’s location in the centre of the country has underlined its importance for nearly two thousand years and contributed to its prosperity. Derby has always been the ‘Crossroads of History.’ Some people went on to greater things, others turned back, some stayed, some died in battle, while others were imprisoned or executed.

Every region in Great Britain has its own folklore, legends and ghost stories and the more I talk to people the more my horizons are being widened. I am continually learning and gaining information that enables me to put another piece of the jigsaw in place as to why and how ghosts may exist. The more research and investigating that I do the greater my quest becomes to prove beyond all doubt that there is life after death and that the dead do return.

The idea of sharing our world, our homes or places of work with the spirits of dead people can be very disturbing, but I have interviewed thousands of ordinary, sane, sober individuals who swear they have encountered a ghost but did not find the experience at all frightening. I believe that the real aim of any ghost hunter should be to see how they can help the ghost and try and discover why they have not 'moved on.' It is important to understand that ghosts – whether the product of the living or the dead – haunt places for different reasons. Some are happy so let them stay but some wish to be released. Their appearance before you is a cry for help from beyond the grave. So for their sake, in fact for everyone's sake, we should be helping them to find release from their earthly torment.

I hope by writing this book I will be able to explain what a ghost really is, what its purpose is and why it is still earthbound. I am by no means an expert. I am just someone who is fascinated by ghosts and someone who has spoken to thousands of folk who have had ghostly experiences. They are not all 'nutters', over tired, drunk, making it up, mistaken, or have a vivid imagination.

As long as there has been life or should I say death on this planet there have been stories of an after life and the dead returning. All the major religions have at their core a belief that each of us has an immortal soul or spirit which survives death. Whether we have an interest in ghosts or not we all have a fear and fascination in death and of course what if anything lies beyond. The only thing in our lives that we know for definite from the day we are born is that one day we are all going to die.

How much proof do we have of life after death? NONE and I will not be able to prove any of it to you. I will offer you some interesting ideas that at least will start some debate, argument, discussion and possibly more research into a subject that has fascinated man-kind since he first set foot on this earth.

TO THE BELIEVER NO PROOF IS NECESSARY. TO THE SCEPTIC NO PROOF IS POSSIBLE.

WHAT IS A GHOST

'From ghoulies and ghosties
And long legged beasties
And things that go bump in the night
Good Lord deliver us.'

The Oxford Compact English Dictionary today tells us that 'a Ghost is an apparition of a dead person that is believed to appear to the living.' To quote The Concise Oxford Dictionary of Current English 1911 a ghost is 'The principal of life, Spirit of God, soul of a dead person in Hades etc, a dead person appearing to the living.' Which of course is absolutely correct, that is what we all think a ghost is. Where did this word originate. This word that sums up everything terrifying, evil, demonic and scary, that appears at two am on a dark windy night in your bedroom when you are alone.

Geist (German) Gast (Old English) Gheest (Flemish) Geasa (Viking), all originate from the primitive Indo European words Ghois or Ghoizdoz meaning terror, frightful, or frightening but also spirit and breathe. This led to the Middle English word Gost (from old English Gast). It became Ghost when William Caxton brought the first printing press to England from Belgium in 1475 and spelt it the Flemish way with a silent H. So that primitive word is used to describe anything and everything that moves without human touch, appears but does not acknowledge, walks through walls, creates noise, combusts without matches, creates anomalies on our digital camera and generally does not conform to our boring ideas of normality. The word Ghost simply means to be frightened and we are frightened (aghast) of what we do not understand.

"*Have you ever seen a ghost? No I haven't, well actually…*" That is how most folk respond to this question. A few years ago I was at a dinner party, it was about 11.30pm, the conversation was struggling a little and people were looking at their watches. The port and brandy decanters were empty and the cigars had been smoked. It was time for an early night until someone said those immortal words, "*Has anyone ever seen a ghost?*" Silence fell over the table for a few moments and then the stories started. More brandy was called for and more cigars came out. We were still sat at the table at 4.30 in the morning. What a way to re-kindle the dying embers of a failing dinner party. Most people if they are honest have had some form of paranormal experience in their life and once prompted are prepared to talk about it.

Before we progress let me tell you that the profession of a ghost (if it had one) is not to scare. Ghosts are not there to 'get you' when you are alone in the dark or at any other time. They are just there. For what purpose we do not know, but what we do know is they are not there to do us harm.

Ghosts have had very bad press over the last two thousand years and remember that history is always written by the victor, i.e. the Church. Many arguments, battles and wars have all been a result of conflict with religion. Through its lust for power and wealth the Church has slowed down the progress of science and shadowed the world from enlightenment. Even to present day the Church refuses to recognise ghosts although it has been responsible for the creation and demonisation of them. So where does our fear come from? I think it originates from primeval fear; it was born into us and has stayed with us from the very beginning. Pre-historic man did not venture into the dark woods at night for fear of what might be lurking behind a big oak tree, i.e. a Sabre Toothed Tiger which would eat him, or a marauding Viking that would hack him to pieces. Due to these threats to his survival he stayed away from the woods and dark places at night. Of course there is always one, the fellow with an extra dose of testosterone who feared nothing. He would venture into the dark woods at the dead of night and guess what happened to him? He got eaten by a Sabre Toothed Tiger. Therefore it is the fear gene that has passed down through the centuries and keeps us alive. It is still with us, just remember the sensation you get when playing hide and seek when the seeker is getting close to you, or how you just do not like to stand with your back facing a dark room. We no longer fear the Sabre Tooth Tiger or the Viking but we still fear the Ghost... partly because we want to. We love the scare factor and Hollywood, M. R. James, Lord Halifax, Edgar Allen Poe, Most Haunted, Living with the Dead etc, have all fuelled our insatiable appetites. I suppose whilst it is scary we will be more fascinated. After all when we go to a theme park we do not choose to go on the ride that takes us round and round on a flat surface. We like to go on the scariest, the one that takes us high into the sky and drops us like a stone. If the ghost programme, book or film was not scary enough we would switch off, put the book down or leave the cinema. Basically we are frightened of anything that we do not understand. Medieval mapmakers would leave large areas of the uncharted world blank or write 'Here there be Monsters.' Although the Greeks knew about it thousands of years ago, up to four centuries ago most of us were terrified of sailing over the edge of the Earth as we believed it to be flat. Imagine Columbus's family waving him off on one of his journeys of discovery, they were not sure if they would ever see him again as he might fall off the edge of the Earth. Today if we venture on a cruise around the world we know we will eventually arrive back from where we started. Sightings of ghosts are reported all over the world and most cultures accept to a degree that the dead can return.

Great Britain seems to be the most haunted country of all and we do seem to take a pride in our haunted locations. There is hardly a castle, stately home, pub or thatched cottage that does not have its' resident ghost. Perhaps it is the influence of the Church of England from 1534 that has had an affect but there is one thing for sure, ghosts are an 'English Speaking Peoples Thing' that is England, Ireland, Scotland, Wales, Australia, New Zealand, America and Canada. Whilst I was on Most Haunted I always tried to carry out extra research before doing a programme. We were in Holland at a castle called Kastille Dorworth. I located a small museum in the town and asked the curator if he had any books on the castle. He went away and came back with a smile on his face. *"Here,"* he said , *"I have found for you the first ever history of Kastille Dorworth written in English," "Great,"* I said, *"does it have any of the ghost stories in it?" "Agh,"* he said *"ghosts are for the English."*

Over the years I have been referred to as the credible one in the Ghost business, I do not see dead people but I do believe there is something in it, but I am firmly sitting on the fence. I am not an expert, I am just a guy that is fascinated by and has a passion for the subject. I have a huge jigsaw puzzle in front of me which is only half complete, but there is not a day goes by when someone does not give me another piece to put into place. 'There is the ghost of a grey lady in that room' is not enough for me. I suppose I have an inquisitive mind. I want to know who she is, why is she grey, why not pink, blue or green? What happened to her to cause her still to be earthbound? Why is she still here? She should have moved on. Do you realise how many people have died on this planet since the beginning of time? Billions and billions and billions. So where are all their ghosts? Well they have all gone. If they were still around we would not be able to see the wood for the trees. The wind would be thousands of ghosts passing us by. Dense fog would be thousands of ghosts all huddled together. It is not like that. Most spirits, souls (ghosts) have gone somewhere. Another spiritual level, another dimension, another frequency, but not Heaven or Hell I am afraid. In other words there has to be a reason why a ghost is still here. Perhaps the way in which it met its' death or the way it lived its' life. Perhaps a fear of what comes next or even a love of what has already been. However, I also believe that eight out of ten paranormal or ghostly occurrences have a logical explanation. What does paranormal mean… running alongside the normal or to quote the dictionary 'beyond normal scientific understanding.' What about supernatural? Well it's just natural but a bit super. There is just not enough research being carried out into the paranormal. Perhaps the reason is that there is little funding set aside for such research. Without money available, enthusiasm and interest in ghosts is not enough to drive investigation forward. Is this the reason why so many scientists do not believe in ghosts? Next time a scientist with letters after their name tell you there is no such thing, tell them this:- For the last four hundred years men with letters after their name (Astronomers) have been peering into the night sky through telescopes looking at dead stars. By the time the image of that dead thing travels the millions of light years to earth all they are looking at is a ghost. Oh! But hang on a minute there are no such things as ghosts.

John Flamstead, first Astronomer Royal. King Charles II had the Royal Observatory at Greenwich built for him. No John Flamstead, no Greenwich Mean Time. He saw ghosts through his telescope.

Although I do not really believe in ghost photography, this is to me the most convincing picture. This photograph was taken in 1936 in Raynham Hall by Captain Provand, a professional photographer. He was taking photographs on the staircase at the hall when this figure appeared. He then took the photograph which later appeared in Country Life Magazine. This figure is almost identical to the one I saw in Derby Gaol.

RECORDINGS

"Occasionally a person appears able to respond to stimuli embedded...among psyco-physicle surroundings, in a manner at present ill-understood and almost incredible.

Take for example a haunted house... wherein some room is the scene of a ghostly representation of some long past tragedy. On a psychometric hypothesis the original tragedy has been literally photographed on its' material surroundings, nay even on the ether itself, by reason of the intensity of emotion felt by those who enacted it; and thensforth in certain persons an hallucinatory effect is experienced corresponding to such an impression. It is this theory that is made to account for the feeling one has on entering certain rooms, that there is an alien presence therin, though it is invisible and inaudible to mortal sense"

(Man and Universe, 1933, Sir Oliver Lodge, 1851-1940. President of the Society for Psychical Research)

My hero, Sir Oliver Lodge. Author of many books on the paranormal and the first person in the world to send a wireless message.

I believe that the vast majority of ghostly sounds and sightings are nothing more than a recording held in the fabric of a building, the soil, rocks, sand, water and the ether. For many years this has been referred to as the Stone Tape Theory. Sand stone, granite and quartz are made of Silica which is a combination of Silicon plus Oxygen (silicon dioxide). Together they make up most of the earth's crust and Silica/ quartz is the most commonly found mineral on the planet. Silica is a very good semi-conductor which means that its' electrical properties can be controlled to regulate the flow of electrons and handle electric currents. What is the memory on your computer stored on? Silicon Chips, Micro chips that hold memory enabling us to record onto them. Could this recording property be present in a stone building?

The redder the sandstone the more iron oxide it contains. This red colouring is what we usually refer to as rust which is magnetic. One hundred years ago we would never have

Chillingham Castle, Could the stone in this building hold a recording of a traumatic and turbulent past.

Mosley Old Hall Wolverhampton. A huge brick tape recorder.

believed that it would be possible to take a strip of sticky silica, sprinkle it with some rust particles and then use it for recording purposes. However, we know that we can… it is a cassette or a video tape. Could this explain why so many castles, stone cottages and stately homes are the scenes of so many paranormal and ghostly experiences? Clay is also made of silica and the redder the clay or brick the more Iron Oxide it contains, which again is potentially capable of holding a recording. In fact it has recently been proved through arcio – magnetic dating that a brick holds a memory of its' birthday. When a clay brick, which contains iron oxide, is fired in a kiln to so many degrees centigrade, it re-aligns itself to magnetic north which itself is forever changing. Then by referring to a chart you are able to date the manufacture of the brick, according to the alignment to magnetic North. When the labourer builds a brick wall he does not realise that he is creating a wall of magnetic bars with positives and negatives, pointing in different directions, which may be capable of holding a recording in exactly the same way as your credit

The wall has been built with magnetic North facing in different directions in the bricks.

card, cassette or video tape does.

Silica and Quartz are one and the same, bearing the same symbol, SiO_2. Quartz crystals have amazing powers and are used for dowsing and healing purposes. Quartz among many other stones has a very symmetric atomic structure. All elements are made up of atoms that are both positively and negatively charged. The bonds that bind these formations cause certain specific vibrations. This is how a quartz watch works as silica is made up of negative oxygen ions and positive silicon ions. Pressing the quartz alters the charge so that the negative ions move towards one side of the crystal and the positive ions towards the other. The opposite faces develop negative and positive charges which can be very powerful. The reverse can happen when applying an electrical charge to a crystal making it vibrate at a natural frequency. The first record player picks up used piezo-electric quartz that generated an electric charge under pressure. The energy field surrounding a person can now be photographed by Kirlian photography and it is always increased when the person is in contact with Quartz or any

Credit card, brick wall, one and the same! Due to the energy (emotion) the charges are all lined up in the same direction, as in a cassette.

other crystal. Silica/Quartz is also comparible with the Aboriginal mystical substance called Maban (Stone of the Sun). The stone /crystals from which wise men obtain their mystical powers, have the ability to store, amplify and transfer thought information through pulsed breath according to an amazing scientist called Marcel Vogle who worked for I.B.M for twenty seven years. He developed magnetic coating for their disc drives and the first Liquid Crystal Displays better known as LCDs, which started his fascination with quartz crystals.

In his experiments with crystals he was able to alter the final form of liquid crystal while focusing on its growth. Vogle a devout Catholic, concentrated on an image of the Virgin Mary for an hour while viewing the growth of a crystal through a microscope. Vogle claimed that the result was a shape recognisable as the Madonna. As the crystals began to melt he said that he witnessed a blue flash of light through the microscope. This was believed to be the transformation of thought information into the crystal. He believed that he had witnessed scientific evidence of the meta-physical power of the mind manifesting itself in a physical form.

Vogle carried out many other tests and experiments to prove that quartz crystals can store our thoughts, in the same way as we can record images and sound with video and cassette tapes. He thought that when a crystal is fully grown it has the ability to be enlivened with human bio - energy by the transfer of thought energy. Vogle also learned that by pointing a quartz crystal at another person it would amplify that person's emotions and thoughts to such an extent that it could put them into an altered state of consciousness.

Iron oxide, electro magnetism, silica/quartz could all play a part in recording highly emotional events or thoughts into the fabric of a building. This recording I believe could be continually re-played over the centuries. This could be similar to playing your favourite video over and over again. However, with continual playing the quality of the recording will deteriorate resulting in the lady first recorded wearing a red dress in 1640 would be seen in 1740 wearing a pink dress and in 1840 wearing a grey dress. In 1940 just a greyish hazy figure would be seen and in 2040 just a faint shadow and a few faint footsteps might be distinguished before the recording fades away completely.

In 1974 physicists at Stanford University created a device that stored information as a hologram within the sub atomic structure of a quartz crystal. They were able to store

Ryton Bridge, West Midlands. Is it the bridge or the water that is haunted?

and retrieve a three dimensional hologram of the Mona Lisa.

Quartz/silica which are both contained in stone and ice have a similar hexagonal geometry. Vogle realised that there is a constant assembling and dissembling of bonds between molecules inside these solids. He spent over a year cutting crystals until he finally created a quartz crystal that resonated at the same frequency as that of water. This he called 'The Tree of Life.' He could then structure water by spinning it around a tuned crystal, altering many of the characteristics of the water and converting it into what he called an 'information storage system.' N.A.S.A. is experimenting with water in space probes as they also believe that water has the ability to hold a memory.

Haunted toilets, Manor House, West Brom.

Just think how many allegedly haunted locations are wet or damp. Riversides, streams, ancient wells, underground springs, marshland, washhouses kitchens, toilets and bathrooms. There are numerous toilet ghost stories that have been told to me over the years. Only a month ago on the York Ghost Walk I was telling the story of a royalist soldier who was killed in a duel by the River Ouse and his ghost is still seen on the river bank. The conversation progressed to the topic of 'toilet ghosts' Afterwards a lady on the walk came to me and said "I am so glad you mentioned that, when I was growing up I thought that all bathrooms came complete with washbasin, toilet, bath and an old lady."

The way in which water is thought to hold a memory is very similar to Homeopathic Medicine, the brain child of German physician Samuel Hahnemann as long ago as 1796. He heavily diluted preparations thought to cause effects similar to the symptoms of various illnesses. While diluting the substance up to thirty times in water, he used a process called succession, (meaning to agitate or shake vigorously) causing an electro magnetic charge to be held in the water which could help to cause some sort of recording.

More credence was given to this theory when a French scientist Professor Jacques Benveniste, was experimenting with antigens which cause allergies. These antigens have to be diluted in water before being administered to a patient, to prevent serious allergic reactions. This actually happened to me when I was being treated for Hay Fever. I was given an antigen which was too strong and as a result my face and tongue swelled dramatically and I was rushed into hospital to be given a dose of hydroquartizone to relieve the swelling. I was then put on a child's dose which had been drastically diluted. By mistake one of Benvenistes' lab technicians diluted the substance so much there was no trace left of the antigen. When it was injected into the recipient it still caused an allergic reaction. Meaning that the water somehow held a memory of what was once in it.

Tom Lethbridge also believed in ghosts being recorded into water. He was a Cambridge Don and Keeper of Saxon Antiquities at Cambridge. He was also an expert dowser and believed that dowsing was in some way a response to the electromagnet field of water. After he and his wife retired to

Devon they had various paranormal encounters which always seemed to be close to water. Both he and his wife saw a ghost by a stream near their home. His wife also had a strange experience at Ladram Beach. First of all she encountered a fog of depression near a stream that ran down from the cliff. When she stood on the cliff the same depression came over her and she sensed someone or something urging her to jump. This sensation had also been experienced by other people. A few years later someone did jump to their death from that spot. Lethbridge speculated that although no-one had committed suicide at the time there was a possibility that someone in a very depressed state stood on that spot contemplating ending it all and left a memory in the damp atmosphere.

Lethbridge was a great believer in Earth energies and believed that the Earths electro magnetic fields centred on natural features such a streams, rivers, underground springs, ancient wells, woods, moor lands and mountains. He believed that strong mental or emotional thoughts could store images at these energetic spots and be replayed to someone passing by years later, perhaps daydreaming or with very little on their mind at the time. Children are often free of worries and are described as having an 'open mind.' He also believed that this was also more likely to happen if the atmospheric conditions were damp and humid.

Lethbridge wrote a series of books on dowsing, earth energies and ghosts. In his book 'Ghosts and the Divining Rod' he gives an insight into a possible ghost sighting. *" Suppose a youth sits down on the bank of a stream, and falls into a vivid sexual daydream in which he imagines a girl taking off her clothes and bathing. His excitement is so strong that his mental image of the naked girl is recorded on the electrostatic field of the water. Some time later a passer by thinking of nothing in particular, catches a glimpse of a naked girl in the stream, a moment later she vanishes. He naturally supposes that she is a supernatural being who has made herself invisible when she sensed she was being watched."*

Tom Lethbridge coined the phrase 'Naiad Field' for the

recording field of water which somehow replays the captured thoughts or emotions through the receiver/ computer /brain of that passer-by as a holographic image. This was actually achieved in 1974 by physicists at Stanford University, America, when they created a device that stored information as a hologram which I mentioned earlier.

Perhaps the water in the well, bricks or the Silica in the stone, or even the water trapped in the oak timbers may act as some form of photographic plate. This could explain hauntings in modern houses that have been built from reclaimed material, as the recording comes with the fabric. It could also go a long way in explaining how ghosts walk through walls, locked doors and appear legless as the building may have changed beyond recognition since the traumatic or emotional recording was originally made.

I believe that it is the electro magnet field in water that gives it the ability to hold a recording. Water also contains at least six percent Silica. As water passes through or over the earth it absorbs dissolved Silica from sand, rocks and minerals. Human beings are approximately seventy five percent water, our brain is eighty five to ninety percent water and we contain seven grams of Silica in our body, more than Iron. As we grow older our Silica intake and retention drops. Could this be the reason why we start to lose our memory. Research in France has proven that adding Silica to our water intake reduces the chance of Altziemers and other degenerative diseases by almost eleven percent.

Our brain is the best computer on Earth. Will the next generation of super computers be made up mainly of water, exactly the same as the one in our skull!

This is all very well but how does the recording take place? You cannot just hold up a cassette or video tape, shout 'abra cadabra' and expect it to record an image. What do you need in your camera, camcorder or tape recorder to make a recording...ENERGY of course! Are you ready for the WOW factor? Every human being emits two kilowatts of electricity in a twenty four hour period. In other words each one of us is a two bar electric fire. We are electric. We are magnetic. We are nothing but energy. It is said that some people have the ability to build up such a powerful electrical charge that anyone who touches them can receive a severe electric shock. I am sure you have heard of the mother who has lifted a car off her trapped child single handed, or other super human feats performed by mere mortals. In 2007 a young Royal Marine was blown up in Afghanistan, his land rover turned upside down in a stream. He was trapped by his seat belt, submerged in water, slowly drowning. Single handed a Royal Marine Sergeant lifted the two ton Landrover out of the stream and saved the lads life. How could he possibly do that? Adrenaline may account for some increase in performance, but not on this scale. He cannot remember doing it, but he has witnesses to prove it and the young marine lived to fight another day.

Three years ago I was talking about super human power in Derby Gaol and there was a chap in the audience who had run over his girlfriend. The car was trapping her by her legs. He lifted the vehicle on his own, releasing his injured girlfriend. However, he could not remember lifting the car. I said to him, *"come on then let's go out to the car park and try it"* His comments to me are unrepeatable but were similar to *"don't be silly I could not possibly do that on my own,"* but he had done just that!

We all have a power reservoir within us that we can harness in times of crisis. We are super humans. We just do not understand the immense power that we can use if the situation arises. We underestimate the capabilities of the human body. We have within us our own energy source, our own battery which every night we lay down to sleep to recharge. What is the biggest crisis that any of us will ever face? DEATH... It is pretty traumatic. I do not mean dying peacefully in a nursing home at a grand old age with all your family around you. I am talking about tragic, traumatic, premature death, such as murders, suicides, accidents, battles and executions. In other words your time had not come and the energy that your body is

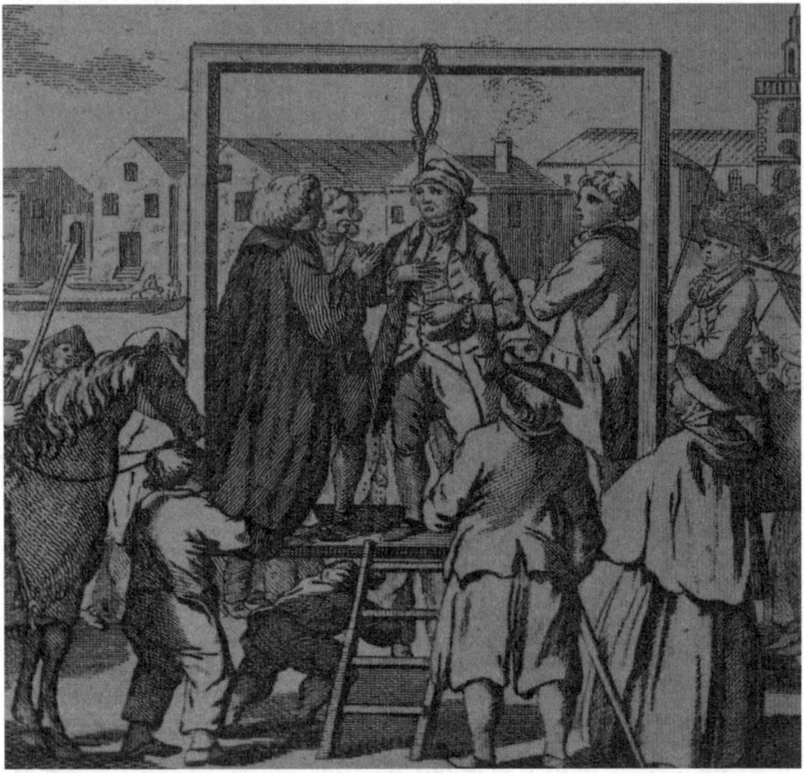

How about this for trauma?

capable of harnessing in order to keep you alive is immense. Just before death a huge surge of electro magnetism is given off from the body which can provide the energy needed to make a recording of us just before we die in the magnetic fabric of the surrounding building. Give this some consideration, why are all ghosts not stark naked? How can you see the ghost of a suit of armour or a Roman helmet when it does not have a soul or a spirit. Is it because they were wearing these items just before they met with their traumatic death which was recorded into the material of the surrounding building? This apparition or ghost is in no way an intelligence and has no way of interacting with us. It does not know we are there. If I were to take you back four hundred years and try to explain to you that I could take a piece of plastic tape, place it in a machine, press the replay button and project the moving image and sound of a person long dead, I would have been dragged away and burnt at the stake. Today if I was to project an image onto a cinema screen of John Wayne dressed just as he was before he died, would it cause the audience to flee the cinema thinking they had seen a ghost? Would the cinema manager call in a group of paranormal investigators or an Exorcist? Of course not, it is just a recording. So if I held up a brick in one hand, a video tape in the other, you would accept the fact that I could record onto the video tape but would you accept that I could record onto the brick? No, not yet but perhaps you will by the time you have finished reading this book.

Richard in front of Treasurer's House. They all say that Borley Rectory was the most haunted house in Britain. Richard disagrees, there is hardly a room in Teasurer's House that does not have a ghost or a ghostly story.

So far we have the Stone Tape Theory, The Water Tape Theory, I think they may be one and the same. Perhaps it should be called 'THE SILICA TAPE THEORY.' There is a story that adds so much credibility to this theory. I believe it to be the best ghost story in the World.

York, 1953, eighteen year old Harry Martindale, a heating engineer was in the cellar of Treasurer's House.

Unbeknown to Harry it was a very haunted building. He was in the barrel vaulted cellar on a small step ladder, drilling a hole through the barrel vaulted ceiling. He was all alone. All of a sudden he heard a trumpet blast, the mind of course has to rationalise what it is hearing, he did not think to himself, *"Oh a Roman trumpet,"* he just looked down the corridor and thought someone has got their radio on very loud. He then heard the trumpet again but this time he could tell that it was coming from the wall in front of him. As he looked down a Roman soldier started to appear out of the wall and as Harry said to me *"What do you do when you are frightened, you step backwards,"* and of course Harry was on a step ladder. He stepped back and fell off the ladder on to the floor. He sat there amazed as about twenty Roman soldiers, two by two, came through the cellar wall towards him. He was terrified. His first comments were to himself, *"Oh my God they are Roman soldiers what will they do to me?"* They did

nothing to him, they did not see him but he could see them. He described them in great detail. The strange thing was that they were little Roman soldiers, they were no more than four feet high and had no legs. He described them in such detail even down to the stubble on their faces. He described their helmets, the small shields, the little swords and the spears that they had got in their hands. At the back of them a Roman soldier on a horse came through the wall and again he was able to describe the horse in great detail. They all passed him without making comment, without looking at him without even noticing he was there and disappeared through the other wall. Harry scrambled to his feet and ran. Halfway up the stairs he bumped into the curator of Treasurer's House who said to him, *"You look as if you have seen the Romans."* Harry turned to him and said, *"Why didn't you tell me?"* He left the building, went back to his yard and told them what they could do with Treasurer's House. He never even got his tools back. On the way home he called at his doctors and the doctor put him on the sick for two weeks with stress. Being an eighteen year old lad Harry told

Richard and Harry on the very spot where he saw the Roman soldiers.

his mates, everybody laughed at him, everyone ridiculed him until eventually Harry stopped telling the story. Do remember this was 1953. Harry went on to be a York City policeman for thirty years, a credible guy, not one to make up silly ghost stories. In the early 1970's they did an archaeological dig underneath Treasurers' House and eighteen inches below the cellar floor they found the Via Decumana, the old Roman road in the same position where Harry had seen his Romans. Those Roman soldiers had their sandaled feet on the original Roman road, probably made of granite, eighteen inches below the present cellar floor which cut them off at the knee and made them appear legless.

Harry is not the only person to see Romans in Treasurer's House. At least five other people have seen them since 1900 and always in the month of February. I believe that what Harry saw on that fateful winters morning was a recording of a tragic and very traumatic incident involving a Roman Patrol heading back towards the Roman Fort they were ambushed by invading barbarians at the end of the Roman occupation of Briton.

I believe that Harry's Romans were nothing more than a holographic recording held in the Silica in the granite Roman road. One thing I have not done is to check how damp the cellar is in Treasures' House. I use this ghost story on every ghost walk, talk, lecture and after dinner speech that I do. Three years ago my youngest son Wills had the opportunity to make a DVD called Ghosts of York. I could not do this without featuring an interview with Harry Martindale. I rang him up and introduced myself and told him what we had planned. He stopped me by saying that he did not talk about the incident at Treasures' House any more as he had recently had serious heart problems after coming out of a lecture that he was presenting about ghosts. I quite understood where he was coming from and said to him *"Thank you for talking to me it has been a real privilege to talk to you as I use your story on every event that I do and can I just tell you that you are my hero,"* the phone went silent for a moment and then this voice said *"Go on then I'll do it."*

He completed the most fantastic interview in the cellar, on the very spot where he saw his ghosts and I asked him at the end of the interview if he believed in ghosts and he said to me, *"Only the ones that I have seen."* To be honest meeting Harry Martindale was the highlight of my ghost hunting career.

Until I was twenty seven I was a ghost virgin as I had never seen or heard a ghost, thank goodness. I was an officer cadet in the Territorial Army and was taking part in a national exercise called 'Exercise Inside Right' at Bestwood Lodge near Nottingham. I have to say it was a spooky place and had been built by King Charles II. We were attacked during the early hours of the morning by The Queens Regiment. I was the radio operator. All my life I wanted to be a soldier and was fulfilling my dreams. I have to tell you I have never been so excited, thunder flashes were exploding, machine gun and rifle fire was all around and I was in seventh heaven. Anyway we won the battle and we all went back to the room where we were going to sleep. It was a large 1930's style conference room and I as radio operator was last one back in with David Freeman, our platoon commander. I got into my sleeping bag up against a wall and settled down but the events of the night were still going through my mind. All of a sudden there was a noise as if someone was coming in and I grabbed my rifle I thought we were about to be attacked again. Nothing happened for a few moments so I put the rifle down and settled back. This voice started up at the back of me. The voice of a young

Above: Bestwood Lodge. Below: Through these doors Richard heard his first ghost.

man, probably seventeen or eighteen, in great pain calling for a nurse, crying, dying. My first thoughts were of course rationalizing what I had heard. I thought it was the chap next to me in his sleeping bag snoring and I have to be honest 'snore, snore' does sound a bit like nurse, nurse but I can assure you it was not. I lay there listening to it and eventually I had tears trickling down my cheeks as I was listening to this young lad dying. The only thing I could not do was press a buzzer to get a nurse because there were no nurses, I was not in a hospital. I did what most people do, I fell asleep but the following morning I was extremely excited to say the least after what I had heard. I told no one. Would you tell thirty seven soldiers that you heard a ghost last night? I was driving a minibus down to Sennie Bridge in Wales for the rest of our fortnight camp together with a soldier called Charlie Zamit from Malta and a young lady that we had given a lift to who was with the Women's Royal Army Corp. We were chatting. She said to us *"where were you, what did you do on the exercise?"* I said, *"Well last night we were in Bestwood Lodge."* *"Oh"* she said, *"that's haunted"* and I said *"wow just a minute, just a minute."* She said *"No honestly there is an article in the Nottingham Evening Post this week about it being haunted"* and I said *"Well just a minute before you say any more Charlie you are my witness to this, was it a hospital during the war?"* She said, *"yes, that was part of the article, it was requisitioned by the Army during the Second World War and used as hospital."* So I believe what I heard that night was nothing more than a recording of this young soldier's last moments before he died. Although I told you I was frightened of ghosts I was not particularly frightened when I heard it, but I was frightened afterwards because I believed that it might have attached itself to me and followed me down to the camp in Wales. I remember walking around alone with a big pickaxe handle at about three o'clock in the morning on guard duty, quite frightened, quite worried thinking has he followed me, but of course he could not, he was a recording. He was encapsulated in the fabric of that building at Bestwood Lodge where that recording is still being replayed over and over and over again. All you need to do is find the right person, the right medium, someone who happens to be tuned in on channel five or whatever to hear him again and I was that person that night. I was tuned into him just once. I have been back to Bestwood Lodge several times since that night in 1976 and even filmed in the same room, but have never heard a thing. Do remember that my mind was in a totally altered state that night after the exercise.

People that are famous and remembered after death have a certain energy, presence and charisma, such as Mary Queen of Scots, who haunts many of the castles in this country where she was imprisoned. However, for some reason she does not haunt the castle where she was executed. When you meet someone like her, you often remark afterwards 'she left a real impression on me' do you think it possible that someone with that much energy can also leave an impression of themselves in the fabric of the building?

A few years ago I had the privilege of visiting the most haunted house in California, the Whaley House. It is the oldest brick building in America, hence the recording side of ghosts. Most buildings in California are wooden therefore they will not contain recordings, but would have spirits, souls and entities that are an intelligence. Britain has mainly brick and stone buildings, therefore we have more ghost recordings.

Mary Queen of Scots.

We now move on to the Spirit, Soul, Consciousness, Energy, Entity, Ego, an intelligence.

CAN THE DEAD RETURN

I believe that the dead can return and I also believe that they can stay around if they so choose. They are seeking some kind of 'closure' as our American cousins would say. They can interact with you, they are aware of the environment in which they and you dwell and they know you are there. They are a conscious entity that can interact with you and speak to you. After death they are still an intelligence. To me they are the most frightening type of ghost and often look like the shades from our worst nightmares appearing as a grey, white or blue haze or fog, person shaped but with no features. It is exactly what I saw in Derby Gaol at twenty past three in the afternoon. Do remember though, that being an intelligence they can also present themselves through your perception as they would like you to see them. Remember that a loved one would not wish to frighten you and they still have an ego which according to the dictionary is, 'the conscious thinking subject.'

Grandpa can appear as you would remember him, dressed in those familiar clothes, before his illness. What though, is the reason for their existence here on earth? Why do they not move on? The basic premise is that the spirit or soul of a dead person moves on to its eternal reward and most do! So maybe our interactive ghosts have unfinished business on Earth that they have not concluded or are somehow trapped and cannot move on to where all good souls should go.

If you can try to imagine how many people have died on this planet since life started, (or should I say since death started), billions, everyone apart from us. Where are their ghosts? They have gone to wherever. Perhaps we should get rid of that concept that they have gone far away from us. All the way up into the clouds to Heaven or all the way down into the fiery depths of the Earth, burning in Hell for eternity. How come nobody ever sees a ghost float past the window when in an aeroplane? Or why don't we see the occasional tormented soul pop out of a volcano? They may well be closer to us than we realise. Dwelling alongside us in another dimension, spiritual plane or frequency. The possible answer to the question, *"can they return?,"* is that they perhaps never left. It should be much easier for them to pop back than we realise as they do not actually have to book a return ticket and apply for time off from harp playing or boiler stoking. Why then can't they let us know that they are ok? I am sure that no one is stopping them. There are no rules or reasons to say we are not supposed to know. There is the possibility that they need a third party to help them communicate, such as a medium, who will tell us that they have Grandma with them and she is ok and that she loves you and everything is going to be ok and that she is waiting for you. They also seem to be able to communicate with some of us in time of crisis /stress / emotional upheaval/ danger and happy events such as a new family arrival.

People have visitations from loved ones for many reasons. Over the years I have spoken to nurses, doctors and nursing home staff that tell me that they know when someone is going to die as a dead member of their family come back for them and is waiting by their bed. The dying person is often aware of their loved one but occasionally they are fighting them off as if they do not want to go. As family life and values disappear and marriage becomes a thing of the past I would imagine that a particular loved one returning for you could become rather complicated. Which wife will it be that comes back for you, the first, the second, your partner, or your mistress? Oh by the way I turned gay and I'd rather my

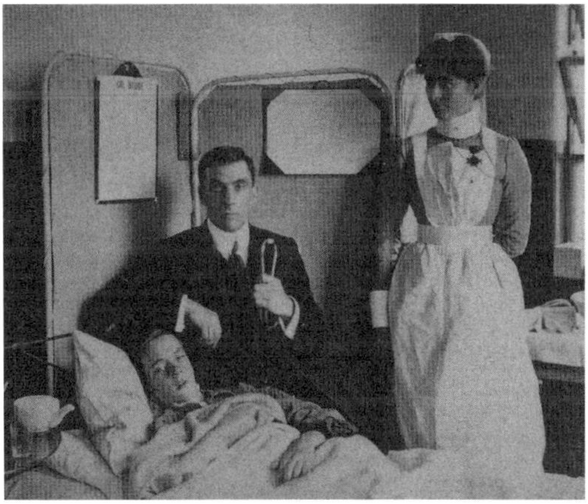

Doctors and nurses know when someone is going to die as someone appeared at the end of the patients bed.

boyfriend come and get me. I have actually been told on good authority that it is the one that you really love and who really loved you that comes back. Many years ago on a Derby Ghost Walk I was told this amazing story by a young lady whose mother died when she was eleven years old. When she was seventeen her father was diagnosed with terminal cancer. Eventually he was taken into the Derby City Hospital and as he deteriorated he was put on a side ward to die. One evening a mate of his from work came to say goodbye. As he approached the drawn curtains he could see the silhouette of a woman at the bedside. He waited outside the curtain and heard the woman saying, *"you cannot come yet the kids still need you."* He recognised the voice as the dying man's deceased wife. His cancer went into remission and he returned home to look after the children for some years.

One of the most frequent sightings is of departed grandparents, witnessed by children who have never known them. The children are rarely frightened and do not flee their bedroom screaming, *"mummy, mummy I've just seen a ghost."* They just say in passing at a later date "*I saw Grandma last night."* Or often when the family are looking at old photographs a child will point to a particular picture and say, *"that's the old lady that comes into my bedroom at night"* and of course it turns out to be Grandma that they never knew.

We also have a phenomenon known as the 'Third Man Syndrome', named after a story in the Bible where Christ appears to two of his disciples on the road to Emmaus and walks along beside them. It has been reported over many years that people in traumatic situations, facing imminent death, have at the eleventh hour found the strength to carry on as they had been aided by the presence of a companion, helper or dead family member. They offered guidance, hope and as a result brought them out alive. These accounts have come from soldiers, World War II airmen, explorers and mountaineers. Many of them being credible people such as Polar Explorer Ernest Shackleton and Aviator Charles Linberg.

In 1947 pilot Bill Cornfield was flying a twin engined

Avro Anson to Singapore when the weather turned. He realised with the amount of fuel in the plane he could neither turn back or reach his destination. In the bad conditions he missed the islands off Greece which would have taken him to a safe landing in Athens. The navigator suddenly noticed the Corinth Canal and Bill took the plane down and pointed it at the mouth of the canal. The mouth of the canyon was very narrow and only a few feet wider than the wing-span of the plane. Flying in a straight line was almost impossible due to the extreme weather conditions. All of the crew noticed a calmness come over the plane as Bill relaxed his grip on the control column and let someone else take over, who landed them safely in Athens. Bill's hero was his elder brother Jimmie who was a Pilot Officer in the RAF during the Second World War. Jimmie was shot down and killed over the North Sea. Bill was convinced that it was Jimmie who took over and flew the plane. Bill stated absolutely and without doubt, Jimmie was with him in the aircraft. He did not see him but knew he was there.

This phenomena has even been referred to in verse by T.S. Elliot in a poem 'The Waste Land':

"Who is the third that walks beside?
When I count only you and I together.
But when I look up ahead at the white road.
There is always another walking beside you.
Gliding wrapped in a brown mantle, hooded.
I do not know whether a man or a woman.
But who is that on the other side of you"

CAN THE DEAD STAY BEHIND

"All houses wherein men have lived and died are haunted houses,"
(Longfellow).

If the dead can return, then there is no reason on earth why they cannot stay around. They are the same as those returning, an intelligence. I personally believe that there are many more Ghosts who choose to stay than those who choose to return, apart from the ones that have had a Near Death Experience, more of that later. Firstly they choose to stay because they want to, because they love the place. Take the old lady who was born in the cottage, lived eighty four years in it, loved it, renovated it, saved up for the pink flock wallpaper in her bedroom and dies in that very room. I frequently have calls from folk who tell me they have moved into a property, been there for about a year and had no problems, then things start to happen. Pictures move, crockery flies and an old lady starts appearing. The first thing I ask is, *"Are you doing any work on the house?"* The usual reply is, *"Oh yes, we have just started*

Richard with a group of ghosthunters outside a haunted cottage.

renovating it and we have also got the decorators in. They have just stripped the awful pink flock wallpaper off one of the bedrooms." Say no more! That was her pride and joy and she really is not happy. *"What can we do?"* They ask. My first comment is do not call in an exorcist, that is just bully boy tactics. Stand in the middle of the house, preferably alone and talk to her. If she is the intelligence that we believe her to be, she will hear you. Tell her it is your house now, and you pay the mortgage. This is a house of the living, not the dead. If you are happy with the situation then tell her you do not mind her being there but please stop throwing things around and do not bother the kids. It can work and what have you lost?

Recently I was in Gloucester at a DVD signing and a gentleman picked up one of my DVDs and said *"I did not believe in any of this stuff until last year my brother moved into our dead mother's cottage on the outskirts of Gloucester. Recently his two little girls have been seeing an old lady in the cottage and on a couple of occasions the lady has climbed into bed with one of the girls. They are not frightened and refer to her as the old lady with black hair and of course most old ladies have grey or white hair."* He went on to say that his mother died at the age of ninety three and still had dark hair. I started to say, *"Is your brother having any..."* when he stopped me and said, *"I know what you are going to say, yes he is having the cottage renovated and my mother does not like what is happening to her home, does she?"*

Another example is when people see a ghost standing by a machine in a factory. The chap that used to work there, spent forty five years at the same machine. He never married, he was always waiting for the factory to open in the morning and he was always the last one to leave at night. He loved that machine, he loved his work, it was his life and when he died he chose to stay. A couple of weeks after he dies the funeral is over and his workmates see him back at the machine, his machine. It is the same with cars. There is a story from America about a pink Cadillac. The owner was a chap who spent twenty five years doing it up, giving it fifteen different coats of paint. He spent all his time in the garage. He loved that car more than his wife and kids and then he died. *"The first thing to go is that damned car."* says the wife, *"He thought more of that than he did of me."* Someone buys the car opens the garage door, looks inside and there is a figure sitting in the driver's seat. It is the old owner, he has chosen to stay with his beloved Cadillac.

There is something about a car that seems to change the male driver into some form of Demon. It is an extension of male ego. Many arguments take place in cars usually caused by the wife complaining about the husband's macho style of driving. It is his domain, his fortress once the doors are locked. He has a secure base in which to attack and the horns immediately start to grow. There is more emotion expelled in a car than anywhere else, apart from a murder site. There are more haunted cars around than we realise. Jane Mansfield, James Dean, Bonnie and Clyde and Arch Duke Ferdinand all died in their cars. These cars are all said to be haunted. Most motor museums have a selection of haunted cars. Are they spirits that are still with the cars or recordings that are held in the Silica found in the steel and paintwork?

In February 1992 my father died, he was eighty three. Like me he was interested in the military, battles, and uniforms and most of the time as a child we would play soldiers. He was very proud of the fact that I went to the Royal Military Academy Sandhurst. Years later we became very friendly with Dr David Chandler, Head of War Studies, R.M.A Sandhurst. Every year I used to borrow some 18th century uniforms from him for the Bonnie Prince Charlie parade that I organised in Derby every Christmas. My father and I would pick them up at the beginning of December and take them back in February. With my father dying in February I delayed taking them back. David eventually rang me in July saying, *"Are you bringing the uniforms back because it will soon be time to borrow them again."* My wife Julia said she would come with me. My brother Peter also offered to accompany me but I said to both of them that I would rather go alone, which I did. When I arrived at the Guardhouse at Sandhurst I had to wait for David to come and collect me from the gates. Just as last year the Ghurkas were on guard duty and I remembered my fathers comments from the previous year when he said to me, *"do you think those rifles are loaded with live ammunition,"* and I said, *"I'm sure they are."* Anyway I stopped daydreaming when David arrived in his car and beckoned me to follow him as usual down to his office. It was approximately a quarter of a mile journey. We both pulled up outside his office. He got out of his car and came over towards me smiling. As I got out of the car to shake his hand he said to me "*Would you and your, oh Richard, I thought you had brought your wife with you but there's nobody there. All the time that you were following me I had you in my mirror and there was someone sitting in your passenger seat and I just presumed it was your wife. You do not think it was father, do you?" "I do not know David,"* I said. I saw nothing but I did move the map book and drinks off the passengers seat on the way home, just in case.

Royal Military Academy Sandhurst, did my father really travel back here with me?

GHOSTS THAT DO NOT KNOW THEY ARE DEAD.

As I sat musing, twas not one but ten-
Rank on rank of ghostly soldiers marching o'er the fen,
Marching in the misty air they showed in dreams to me,
And behind me was the shouting and the shattering of the sea.
(Walter de la Mare 1873-1956.)

Probably the nearest Hollywood film to portray the truth about ghosts is 'Ghost' starring Patrick Swayze. When Sam was shot he was walking up to people in the street trying to communicate with them, not realising that he was dead. I believe that parts of the film are very close to the truth but that is for another book. I think that the main reason for not knowing you are dead is the nature and the speed in which you meet your death. There are numerous Second World War airfields around the world haunted by young airmen who just do not know that they are dead. Imagine an eighteen year old trainee pilot smashing into the ground at three hundred and

Wigsley control tower, Lincolnshire. Gaunt, empty, full of weeds and ghosts of many young airmen.

fifty miles per hour in his Spitfire. Nothing left of him and very little of his aircraft but there he is dazed, confused and dead, wondering what on earth hit him, just like Sam he is wandering around, not the streets but the crash site. *"Where am I, what happened, where's my Spitfire, where's my body?"* He is destined to spend the rest of eternity wandering around the site of the accident or walking across the apron of the airfield towards guess where? The Control Tower for help. Does he think that the war goes on forever?

Battlefields have all the ingredients to cause hauntings.

One of the most underrated places for hauntings are battlefields but they have all the ingredients for causing ghosts; tragic, premature, and traumatic death. Ghosts and history go together. You cannot study ghosts and apparitions without exploring history. It is impossible to stand on a battlefield where thousands of soldiers have died or suffered untold anguish, without feeling a very special something. If you stand very still and listen to the wind whistling over the desolate battlefield you may well still hear the jubilant cries of the victors and the faint melancholy cries of pain and despair of the defeated. We should all stand upon these hallowed sites and give a thought to the ordinary soldier who was prepared to give his life for his King, his regiment, his colours. He believed that fifty yards of tactical ground was worth the sacrifice of his life but he always had the comfort of knowing God was on his side. What about the opposite forces, wasn't god on their side too?

When a soldier gives up his life for a cause that he believes is worth more than his very existence, a recording can

Soldiers of the Rifle Brigade at the beginning of the First World War.

be left behind in the soil or in the building where he died. Spectral battles in the sky, phantom soldiers locked in battle, lone sentries and pathetic cries for help have been witnessed on many bloody battlefields around the world. Surprisingly enough many battles over the centuries were fought during electric storms or in damp conditions and all of them without exception have rivers, streams, marshland and wells on location. The battle is often replayed over and over again years later to terrified onlookers. Obviously with so much death, suffering and trauma in a concentrated area, a memory or recording of the incident can often occur. Many tormented souls linger on the battlefield still waiting for their body to be discovered so that they can receive the Christian burial that they have been denied.

Battlefields in the past have never been top of the list for hauntings. I believe they are underestimated in the ratings. Everything that can cause a ghost is present on the battlefield. These being emotion like no other, fear, jubilation, murder,

The site of The Battle of Sedgemoore on location for filming of Battlefield Ghosts. On 25th July 1685 the Protestant Duke of Monmouth and his pitchfork army met the disciplined forces of the Catholic King James II. Monmouth's troops were slaughtered and the Duke was beheaded, his ghost amongst others still haunts the battlefield.

mass murder, and suicide. Bodies being blown to pieces and soldiers crawling away whilst calling for their mothers, to die alone, often resulting in their bodies never being found. Battlefields were not talked about much as being haunted because very few people lived on them. Apart from the dog walker and the tourist most of them remained uninhabited. Is this why ghosts were not reported as they are in towns and cities? Then came re-enactment thanks to America leading the way, we of course followed. The number of re-enactors that see ghosts is amazing.

They seem to act as trigger objects in the same way as a paranormal investigator will leave a teddy bear in a room haunted by a child, in the hopes it will attract the ghost. Imagine a young Confederate soldier, all of his life in front of him, blown to pieces at Gettysburgh and does not know that he is dead. He has spent the last one hundred and fifty years wandering the now deserted battlefield looking for his regiment. Suddenly he spots a group of grey clad soldiers. His mates, his regiment, he has found them at last, but alas they are not of his world. Do they appear as ghosts to one another? Perhaps they do!

I have recently been making a pilot for a TV series called 'Battlefield Ghosts' with Derek Acorah, Steve Parsons and my eldest son Edd, which is directed by my youngest son Wills, who has his own production company. I think that we would all agree that to spend nights and days on hallowed ground that has soaked up so much blood, been witness to so much emotion and is the final resting place of so many brave souls, has to be one of the highlights of our ghost hunting careers.

Derek Acorah pointing towards the lost mass burial grounds on the battle-field at Sedgemoor.

End of a wet days filming!

GHOSTS OF THE LIVING.

Fifty per cent of all ghost sightings are of the living! There are various categories of this phenomena:

CRISIS APPARITIONS

The vast majority of crisis apparitions tend to have tragic overtones and are associated very much with wars and battles. There are many reported sightings of soldiers, airmen and sailors who have appeared to their mothers and wives, either at the moment of their death or sometimes just before death. They often appear at the foot of their mother's bed but are also seen wherever the loved one is at the time of the tragedy. The dying person seems to be able to telepathically project their image, sometimes thousands of miles from a faraway battlefield or disaster zone to a loved one back home.

I had the privilege of investigating one such incident in Ireland at Castle Leslie, in County Monaghan. The most famous ghost in the castle is Captain Norman Leslie of the Rifle Brigade who was killed only two months after the First World War had started. Two days before he was killed his mother was asleep in the Red Room in the castle when she was awoken by someone in the room. She rubbed her eyes and then realised that it was her son Norman. He was busily going through some papers in a bureau by the window. She spoke to him saying *"Why Norman, what are you doing here"?* He did not speak but looked up at her, smiled and disappeared. This was two days before he was killed in action at Armentieres on 18th October 1914. He was seen again on the day of his death by the gamekeeper standing near the lake in the grounds of the castle. Six weeks after his death his brother Shane went over to France and found what he believed to be Norman's body in a temporary grave. Norman had a broken tooth and his brother put his finger in his mouth to prove it was him by feeling his broken tooth. A few years ago Sammy Leslie was going through some documents, including Norman's will, when a strange sensation came over her and a scrap of paper dropped out from the bundle of documents. Sammy believes this is what Norman was looking for in his mother's bedroom two days before his death. This piece of paper helped solve a family mystery. A few years ago Norman's sword was found on the battlefield and is now a prized possession at Castle Leslie. I had the honour to conduct a séance at the castle with Norman's sword by my side. In the past his ghost was often seen by guests staying at the castle but he did not come through that night. Perhaps he is now at rest after the family mystery has been solved.

Norman Leslie's temporary grave.

Captain Norman Leslie, Rifle Brigade killed Armentieres
18th October 1914

Norman Leslie's letter home just before he died:

'Try not to worry too much about the war. units and individuals cannot count. Remember, we are writing a new page of history. Future generations cannot be allowed to read of the decline of the British Empire and attribute it to us. We live our little lives and die. Some are given the chance to prove themselves men, and to others no chance comes. Whatever our individual fault or virtues matter little, for when we are up against big things we must forget the individual. Some will live and many will die. We cannot count the loss. It is far better to go out with honour than to live with shame.'

PHANTASMS

Phantasms are not ghosts of dead people. They are named after the great S.P.R study (Society for Psychical Research) 'Phantasms of The Living' are 'ghosts' of people who are very much alive and well. They can be generated in many ways, but again mainly by telepathic projection. Sometimes not due to any sort of tragic incident but more by just thinking of someone or somewhere or just daydreaming can result in the projection of an image of ourselves.

A famous case involved a village baker in the 1960's who retired and sold the shop. Not long after the sale the new owner was intrigued by sightings of the old man's ghost going through all the motions of baking bread. One day the ghostly sightings ceased and the old man was never seen again. At the time the old man was seen haunting his old bakery he was alive. Unable to sleep in the early hours of the morning and not able to adjust his body clock he would get up make himself a cup of tea, sit by the gas fire and daydream about being back in his bakery making bread. Only after he died did his apparition disappear.

ARE POLTERGEISTS DEAD OR ALIVE?

In his book Disquisitionum Magicarum, written as long ago as 1599, Martin Del Rio a distinguished and well educated Jesuit tells of eighteen types of demon. The 16th kind being : *"those spectres which in certain times and places or homes, are wont to occasion various commotions and annoyances. By what arrangement demons can throw stones and perform other things of kinds which seem to require hands and bodily instruments, the scholastics dispute. I agree with those who hold these things to be done by a demon substantially present in*

that place and moving the air next to the stone by a command of will."

The Demons referred to above are very different to the other seventeen demons in Del Rio's book. They really did exist and most disturbing of all they are still with us! Personally I do not believe in Demons as you will find out in the next chapter. In the 21st century we do not believe in or fear demons of Earth, air, fire, and water, demons which shun the light or subterranean demons. Most of us are frightened of Poltergeists but we should not be afraid, just as other ghosts, they are not here to 'get us'.

Partly to blame for our fear is Harry Price, allegedly one of the greatest authorities on ghosts, who wrote 'Poltergeist Over England' (1945): *"A Poltergeist is an alleged ghost, elemental, entity , agency, secondary personality, intelligence,*

Paranormal investigator Harry Price.

power, spirit, imp, or familiar with certain unpleasant characteristics. Whereas the ordinary ghosts of our story books are a quiet, inoffensive, timid, noiseless and rather benevolent spirit, with usually friendly feelings towards the incarnate occupants of any place where it has its abode. The Poltergeist is just the reverse. According to the many reports of its activities, in all lands and in all ages, the Poltergeist is mischievous, destructive, noisy, cruel, erratic, thievish, demonstrative, purposeless, cunning, unhelpful, malicious, audacious, teasing, ill disposed, spiteful, ruthless, and resourceful. A ghost haunts, a Poltergeist infests. A ghost likes solitude, a Poltergeist prefers company. A ghost seeks the half-light; a Poltergeist will perform in sunlight."

Not only Harry Price (who has been accused of being a pathological liar) but also scary movies have given people a very definite idea of what Poltergeists are supposed to do. We have been drip fed an image of evil, mischievous spirits hurling objects at people, showering them with stones or dragging folk out of bed in the middle of the night.

The word Poltergeist is derived from the German verb 'polter', meaning to create noise and the noun 'Geist' meaning ghost. Obviously going back to our Saxon roots. Another word of equal antiquity is Rumplegeist meaning jolting or rumbling spirit, but Poltergeist has become more or less standard English terminology. I was told by a recent visitor to Germany that they still refer to children making a noise as 'poltering.'

There are two contrasting schools of thought on exactly what makes a Poltergeist. Once again the definition comes down to the battle between the living and the dead. One side of the argument believes that they are mischievous spirits, who inhabit a place or room. The other side goes with the theory of Recurrent Spontaneous Psycho Kinesis, RSPK for short. They believe that living people, for reasons we do not understand, use the power of their own minds to effect their environment.

Many Poltergeist cases over the centuries have centred on pre-pubescent children, especially girls. Examples are; the

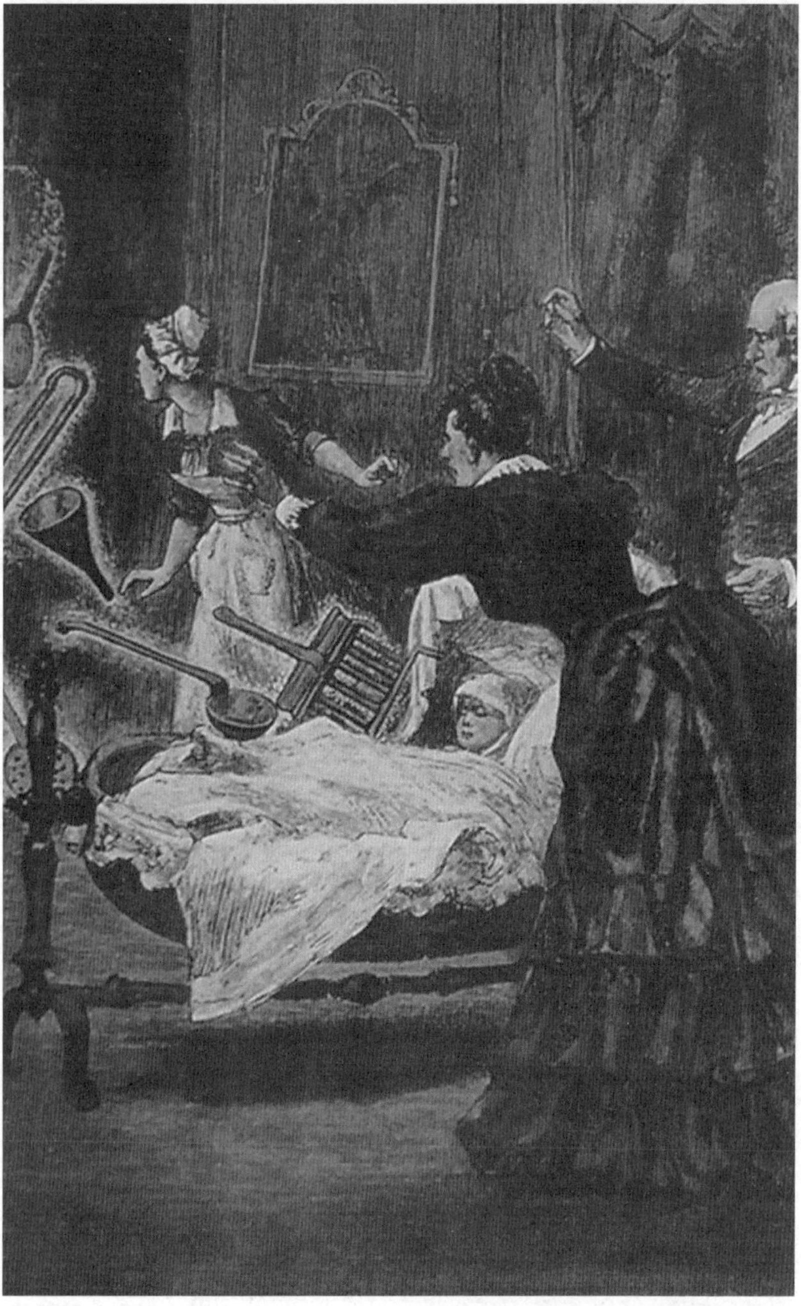

Typical Poltergeist activity, usually attributed to children.

Schiel case in Germany in the 1580's, the North Aston case, 1590's, Epworth Rectory, 1716, Cock Lane, 1760's, Bell Witch, 1817, the Stans case Switzerland, 1860 and the Enfield case, 1970's. Most of these famous cases involved taps, raps and movement of objects. In modern times Poltergeists have discovered that there is fun to be had with electric light bulbs, phones and computers.

It is possible that a living human, not a spirit may be responsible for the Poltergeist activity. In a nutshell this means someone near the site of activity is controlling the matter with their mind. In other words they are the Poltergeist themselves. They are the energy. They are creating the chaos, they are the unwitting cause of the things that happen around them and have no conscious control over them.

The phenomena caused is in some way or other the outcome of a highly emotional state or conflict which has been denied. In some way emotional tension, anxiety, aggressive urges or suppressed sexual excitement generate the energies which exhibit them in what we refer to as Poltergeist activity.

A very interesting case took place in 1975 when a brand new shopping centre opened in Derby. Within days of opening alleged Poltergeist activity was reported from various shops. Some of the phenomena were only experienced at weekends when a large percentage of staff were school children and students. A great deal of joking took place at first but fear soon started to spread. The information was partly repressed for fear of an adverse effect on sales within certain chain stores.

It was around this time that the borough council decided that professional help was needed. All staff were advised to keep a record of events and report any strange occurrences to the council. The outbreak became so serious that exorcisms were carried out in the basements of some shops and Derby Borough Council issued a pamphlet to the shop workers entitled 'Your Poltergeist and How to deal With It'.

The following is an excerpt:

A:Its'History

1. ***Poltergeists are quite common and have been recorded for many hundreds of years.***
2. ***At present cases are being researched and documented in the United States where the work of Dr Rhine of Duke***
3. ***University, and of Roll and the Morrises in England is noteworthy.***

Many people down the ages and many people today, have and are suffering from pranks of their poltergeist.

B: Its Nature

4. It is not an illusion and can produce physical effects which can be weighed, measured and recorded: i.e. it can move things and it can produce noises…

5. It is attached to and part of the mind of an owner or group of owners…

6. The poltergeist feeds on fear, although it is harmless both to soul and body and is, in its own way, a relief to the suffering mind.

7. Its owner has no control over it and is unaware of his or her ownership.

C: How to deal with it.

8. Once the pressures which have produced it are understood, the Poltergeist will fade out.

9. Where premises have been affected; a ritual blessing will greatly help to calm the atmosphere of strain and fear.

Many members of staff from several shops experiencing the phenomena did make themselves familiar with the pamphlet, the phenomena still continued. More exorcisms took place but the Poltergeist activity continued for some time afterwards. Psychotherapy was used on some staff members with positive results which proves in some cases that it can banish Poltergeist activity. If it is right to look to the person concerned for the source of the phenomena, then we may be able to discover why it suddenly ceases. Perhaps some change in their emotional or mental state could mean he or she is no longer producing the extra quantities of energy and therefore the rappings, levitations and stone throwing will naturally stop.

In any event, the mind over matter theory is not endorsed by all investigators. Some believe that only a proportion of Poltergeists can be explained away in this fashion and the reason that the activity stops is because the malevolent spirit gets fed up packs its bags and goes 'home'!

Poltergeists tend to frighten folk more than any other form of ghost. Everyone thinks that they are noisy, mischievous, playful and of course evil. They drag people out of bed, throw furniture around and lift people off the floor. These things have happened but it is very seldom that I have heard of anyone being hurt. Most of the items thrown tend to miss anyone in the room. In fact the projectiles usually veer off just before making contact with an individual as if re-directed by unseen hands. I do not think they want to hurt anyone, I do not think that they are aiming the projectile at you. I think that it might be a cry for help from a spirit or entity that is for some reason trapped on this Earth or plain. They cannot summon up enough energy to materialise or speak but can gain the energy from somewhere to move or throw things, tap or rap on something. They do not mean you any harm they are just trying to get your attention.

So in other words they could be dead people trying to make contact with the living. They are an intelligence communicating with us. In many cases during investigations I have heard raps, taps and bumps. Is this them trying to get our attention by throwing or moving something? Where do they get the energy from? I believe they get it from us, an agent. They use the energy of people, usually a young person reaching puberty, more often than not girls, although there are cases where a grown man is involved. Such a case was reported in the 17th century; 'The Drummer of Tedworth'. In some way emotional tension, anxiety or suppressed sexual excitement generates the energies which the Poltergeist can harness. There are often Poltergeist cases reported in house holds where there is emotional upset, arguments and pending divorce.

A recent case I investigated in Derbyshire involved a farm house where a chap called Clive had lived all his life. As far as he was concerned the house was not haunted. He then moved in his partner with her nine year old daughter. The haunting started. Pictures started moving and falling off walls and the family dog would scratch at the kitchen door trying to get out in the middle of the night. The following morning he would always be found cringing in the corner of the kitchen, staring at what no one else could see. At the same time as this paranormal activity the little girl started talking about 'Mr Ghost' who lived under her bed. While she was in the house she was always tired, lethargic and seemed drained of energy. When she went to stay at Grandpa's house she again became a happy, energetic little girl. Something in the farmhouse was draining her of energy. Clive brought in The Church, Exorcists and paranormal investigators, but the activity continued.

In many cases of hauntings where there is an entity, which is an intelligence, they often draw the energy from the atmosphere i.e. heat. This is why you often get a drop in temperature in a room where a spirit is trying to materialise or make itself known to you in some way. Somehow, I still do not know how, it has the ability to draw the heat or energy in the room towards itself which causes the manifestation. I think that if there is not that much energy in the room you only tend to see head and shoulders of the apparition. When the energy is used up, the apparition vaporises and vanishes. It is a bit like pulling out a 13 amp plug.

In Poltergeist cases the entity tends to attach itself to the mind of an owner or an agent, who of course is also a source of energy (two kilowatts).

There is another theory that Poltergeists are ghosts or spirits of children, hence the fact they tend to be playful, mischievous, sometimes spiteful and spontaneous and of course prone to latching themselves onto or hanging around other children, as if they are still alive. If Poltergeists exist on their own then they may want to attach themselves to a person from this life, so if Poltergeists really are spirits of children then it seems logical that they would attach themselves onto someone of a similar age and mentality. Just cast your mind back to when you were a child. Did you have an imaginary friend, and if you did how old were they? Thirty five percent of children under the age of six have imaginary friends. Well that is what Mum and Dad call them anyway.

SPONTANEOUS HUMAN COMBUSTION

" Call the death by any name...attribute it to whom you will... it is the same death eternally-inborne, inbred engendered in the corrupt humours of the vicious body itself, and that only—spontaneous combustion, and none other of all deaths that can be died"

Charles Dickens 1853

Spontaneous fires are often associated with Poltergeist activity. These cases are often attributed to a particular form of fiery spirit. In these instances the focus of the outbreak, usually but not always, is a child. Children sometimes live through a phase which is often quite brief, during which they appear to have the ability to set nearby objects on fire.

There are many, many recorded instances of spontaneous fire throughout history. One famous case occurred in the Ukraine in 1987. In the presence of a 13-year-old boy, clothes, furniture, carpet and electrical equipment burst into flames for no reason. These frightening outbursts, over 100 in number, began in November 1986. The boy was taken to hospital for observation and tests, whilst there the clothing of the boy sharing his room burst into flames. For a few days wherever the boy went objects flew around and light bulbs exploded.

Spontaneous fires are one thing but cases of Spontaneous Human Combustion (SHC), is the terrifying phenomenon

There are many recorded instances of Spontaneous Human Combustion, if we are pure energy then is it not just possible that this could realistically happen?

where a human literally bursts into flames, it happens without any warning or any form of external ignition. In a very short period they are reduced to a pile of ashes. It is something that has baffled so called scientists for many centuries. Most of them totally disregard the idea and most medical books do not even mention the subject. Yet over many centuries, hundreds of cases of mysteriously charred bodies and piles of human ashes have led many credible witnesses, including doctors, ambulance personnel, fire-fighters and police to come to only one conclusion, nothing could have caused the effects they witnessed other than Spontaneous Human Combustion.

Charles Dickens was fascinated by the subject as long ago as 1853 when he featured a case of SHC in his novel 'Bleak House,' when he killed off the character Krook, Chancellor of the rag and bone department in a classic case of Spontaneous Human Combustion. This fictional death in the book was based on facts. In 1833 when Dickens was a young newspaper reporter working for The Morning Chronicle he attended an inquest on a victim of SHC. Dickens was totally convinced by the reality of the phenomenon. In fact in the preface of 'Bleak House' he actually cites thirty different press reports of death by SHC. Dickens was not the only credible writer to believe; at least eight other distinguished writers included SHC in their pre 1900 novels. Many sceptics have tried to provide rational explanations for SHC with some success but there are still many grey areas that require further investigation and understanding.

I have to be honest I am very sceptical,. How can someone who is seventy five percent water catch fire and continue to burn until nothing remains but a pile of ash? Even more strange is that in most cases of SHC flammable material near to the body such as wood, furniture and carpet all highly flammable have not been burnt. To destroy a body in a crematorium a temperature of at least 3000°F should be maintained for several hours and even then some bones will not have been destroyed. Yet in the case of SHC victims bones have been reduced entirely to ashes. So what on earth (or not on earth) fuels the complete burning of a SHC victim? Some say that a huge leak of body fat acting as a wick, similar to an oil lamp, can fuel the fire. Others say that anaerobic fermentation within the gut can produce large amounts of flammable gases within the body, such as methane and hydrogen but I would have thought this more likely to cause an explosion rather than an uncontrollable fire.

Researchers Vincent H Gaddis and Ivan T Sanderson came up with an interesting theory of events that could lead to an outbreak of SHC. It starts with loneliness, illness or some form of emotional affliction, which leads to a negative state of mind. This emotional state can effect the victim's metabolism to such an extent that phosogens build up in their muscle tissue. Phosogen is not unlike glycerine, which is extremely explosive. Electricity generated by intense sunspots, electric or magnetic storms and electrical energies created by geological activity could trigger the combustion. It could also be possible that high geomagnetism forms ball lightning which can create short radio waves similar to microwaves. Some SHC victims appear to have burnt from the inside outwards. Quite a number of SHC occurrences do coincide with local peaks in the Earth's magnetism. Perhaps we do create the fire from within, just remember that we are pure energy we do not plug into an external energy force, we are our own generator, or Manipura Chakra. This is a fire centre which according to oriental medicine and acupuncture is located in the solar plexus. Every human emits over two kilowatts of electricity each day, we have superhuman power, we are capable of almost anything. Many yoga devotees can stimulate their chakra to such an extent that they glow in the dark. In the Tibetan practice of Tumo, students of the art can generate so much internal heat while in a state of trance that the snow melts around them. It has often been stated that SHC victims seldom cry out or struggle while they are burning as if they were in a state of trance themselves.

Whether we are really capable of self-combusting I am not sure. I am not an expert I am just trying to piece together the many pieces of a large jigsaw puzzle. I believe we have powers way beyond our expectations. We are pure energy and you cannot destroy energy, you can only alter its state. We cannot be destroyed and I do believe we go on to something else.

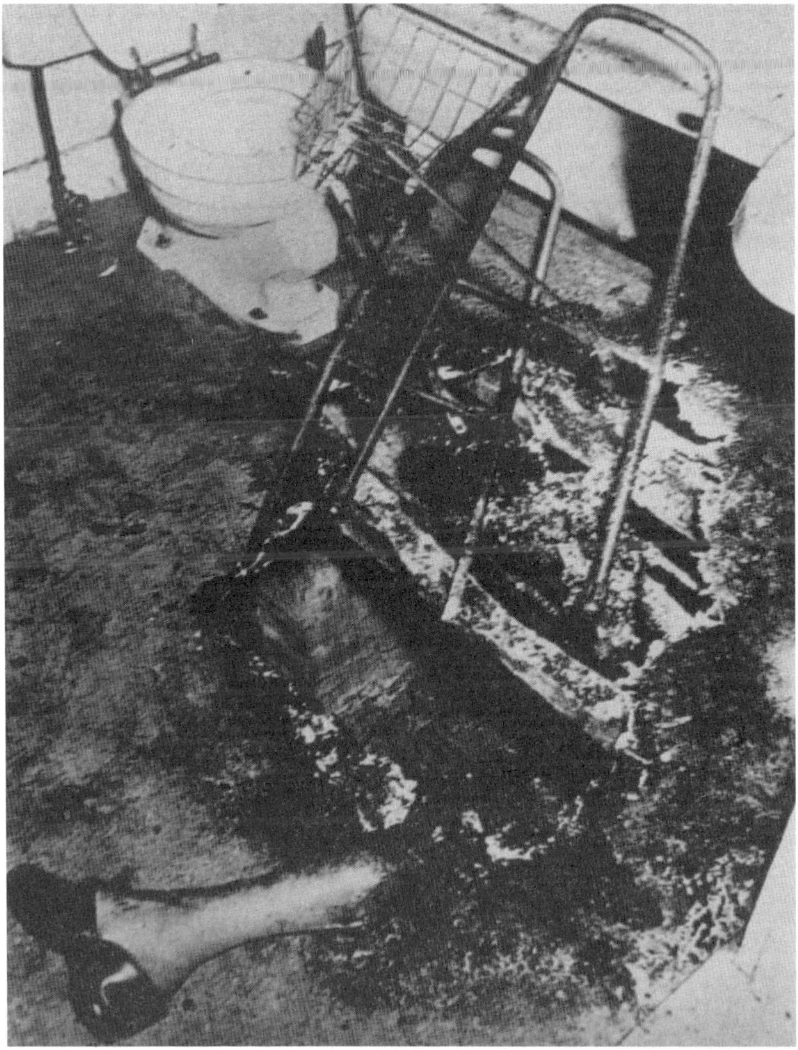

Typical example of Spontaneous Human Combustion.

GHOSTS AND THE CHURCH

Hell is a pit full of horror and misery and all that the tongue can tell is a mere particle of what the condemned shall suffer. For they shall have weeping and gnashing of teeth, a stink in their noses, a voice full of sighs and terror in their ears ferrers on their hands and feet and a burning fire in their limbs.

Four last things 1482 Vier Uterste

Have you ever heard of the ghost of a cave man, a stone age man, bronze age, iron age? No you probably have not. Imagine the headlines in a National Newspaper…

'POT HOLERS SEE GHOST IN PRE-HISTORIC CAVE.'

The ghostly image in the cave exclusively captured by our photographer!

Potholers in Derbyshire yesterday broke into an undiscovered cave and saw a cave man with long hair, dressed in animal skins carrying a club and dragging his wife across the floor by her hair. The terrified potholers watched in amazement as the two pre-historic apparitions walked through the wall of the cave and vanished. A spokes person for the Peak District Rangers said *"We knew that these caves had*

been inhabited in the Neolithic Period as primitive paintings are still preserved on the walls but no one has ever reported seeing the ghost of a cave man before"

Next question. Have you ever heard of the ghost of a youth wearing a baseball cap, a hoodie and his backside hanging out of his jeans, smoking a joint, walking through an apartment wall? No you probably have not. I am not saying that there are no ghosts of cave men. In fact there is a well documented sighting of a Stone Age man according to a Dictionary of Ghosts by Peter Haining, which stated that a figure clad in furs, gallops on horseback across Cranborne Chase in Dorset, brandishing what appears to be a stone axe. The Greeks, Egyptians and all ancient civilisations have reported or believed in the dead returning but not in the numbers that we seem to experience during a certain period of our history.

I am not saying that there are no modern ghosts but there are far less reported sightings of them than Medieval, Tudor, Georgian, Victorian and Edwardian ghosts. WHY?

What raised its ugly head on this planet nearly two thousand years ago? Do not say religion because we have had lots of religions for thousands of years. CHRISTIANITY was established as the Roman Church by the Emperor Constantine. I believe that he actually remained a Pagan for the whole of his life. What he saw in this latest form of religion was a way of controlling the population, not with swords and spears but with fear. What he created was Imperial Christianity, which even depicted Jesus Christ dressed as a Roman Centurion. Christianity became the only legal religion in the Roman Empire and became all powerful. This of course was a terrible blow to all the Pagans that were quite happily worshipping the Sun and Moon, dancing around naked, talking to the trees and being at one with the earth. The word Pagan is derived from the Latin word paganus which means 'country dweller'.

Emperor Constantine, it's all his fault.

Paganism is probably the world's oldest religion. It predates Christianity by thousands of years. It had no evil, there was no such thing as God or the Devil, Heaven or Hell. Life operated in cycles and was itself a cycle. All objects around us, Sun, Moon, Stars and all the forces of nature were part of this life force and was worthy of our respect, we were at one with the Earth. We came from Mother Earth and would return to it.

Unlike Christianity which was male dominated the old religion gave woman an exalted position as a fertility goddess and had a great belief in the wisdom of women. To keep an even balance there was also a horned hunter god, male of course.

Those who knew how to interact with the powers of the Earth were considered the wise ones, the cunning ones. The wise ones of the village who practised nothing more sinister than curing people through a knowledge of herbs, drugs, the workings of nature, ESP, and psychology through the clever use of incantations and the use of rhymes and prayers to invoke a certain reaction in people.

The wiccan or wise one of the village.

Here in lies the key to what has been called the old religion. It was a cult of the wise and in Celtic referred to as 'Wicca Craft'. The emphasis was put more on the feminine side of life and the mother Goddess was worshipped. The Pentagram etched in blood in so many horror films is nothing more than the Pagan symbol for the feminine side of nature. Christianity fed on fear and soon gained power and control. It started hi-jacking the old religious festivals and beliefs to help convert its' more stubborn adherents. What the church could not convert or steal, it demonised. The horned god of hunting was turned into the Devil, the mother goddess was demoted, and the church became a male dominated institution and sex became a dirty word. In fact no-one had fun and nobody talked to the trees anymore. Everything that country folk did was looked upon by the Church as suspicious. They would gather together to celebrate the four main festivals which were; May Eve, Lammas, All Hallows Eve, and Candlemas. The most famous being All Hallows Eve which celebrated the Harvest Festival. This was the end of a very busy time in the countryside and so it was a chance to celebrate the end of hard work and to enjoy

The horned Hunter God turned into the Devil.

some of the 'fruit of their labours.' At this time in the year the days were growing shorter and the Sun God seemed to die. To compensate for this loss of light they lit bonfires to try and entice the Sun to return. Do remember that the followers of the old religion were originally an agricultural cult whose daily lives and survival relied on the fields and the farm. These gatherings were known as 'Covens' just another word for a convention, a meeting or a community or brotherhood. The festivals were known as Sabbats and Esbats and were celebrations of the full moon. These folk knew only too well that the magnetic power of the full moon greatly increased the extra sensory perception of mankind. They believed in Ley Lines and Earth energy which they harnessed for their own physical and spiritual benefit by building temples and stone circles at significant points along the energy lines. Just in the same way as the Chinese do with pagodas and the

Esbats and Sabbats as depicted by the Church. These were nothing more than meetings and celebrations by country folk.

acupuncturist works on the human body.

The Christian Church came along and hi-jacked many of the Pagan sacred sites, built churches on them, cut and pasted their religious festivals and called them HOLIDAYS! Even the Vatican is built on a Pagan site.

In the old religion women carried a broom, a symbol of domestic order and cleanliness. As these women came from the villages and remote farmhouses their brooms were part of their everyday tools. Even the old English word for these superstitious country folk, who clung longer to the worship of nature, was perverted by the church and 'villein' became a villain. The old religion had always believed that mans body contains a power reservoir, which could be used by the coven or community to create a power concentration similar to that of prayer in a church with a full congregation. Psychic ability was always highly rated amongst the Wiccans, and so mediums were considered to be carrying out the work of the Devil. Psychic or sensitive people doing unusual things within the community were dangerous radicals. Any competitor who the church could not control had to be destroyed.

The personification of evil. The Phoenician deity Beelzebub was the Church's model for the Devil, but he was not scary enough, so he was given red skin, cloven hooves , a tail, horns and a pitch fork. No wonder medieval man was terrified.

The dictionary definition of a heretic is *"someone who has an unorthodox opinion."* In the thirteenth century the Roman Catholic Church waged a war against all heretics who were becoming disaffected by the bigoted greedy Roman Church. During this period torture and execution were rife throughout Europe, which was in a pretty bad state, with constant warfare, slavery and lack of communication. People were starting to doubt certain Christian doctrines. Crusades were organised by the Pope but not against other faiths such as Muslims but against fellow Christians who dared to question certain details of their religion. Waldenses and Albigenses who were sects who only differed slightly from the Churches doctrines, in as much that they disliked the pomp and ritual of the Roman Catholic Church and questioned its' right to religious rule. These folk were mercilessly exterminated on the orders of the Pope. Any scientists with radical ideas had to go before a board of inquisitors. Galileo who came up with the theory that the Sun did not revolve around the Earth, was imprisoned. Charles Darwin who was a Christian held onto his theories for fear of persecution and has only just received an apology from the Church of England. The Inquisition or Holy Office gained momentum during the thirteenth century leaving a trail of destruction all over Europe. It was the brain child of Pope Gregory IX who believed that anyone who veered away from the Catholic Faith should die.

Pope Gregory IX

Due mainly to lack of sanitation and pestilence, plague spread throughout Europe killing over a third of the population. The Church blamed it all on God's anger at allowing heresy to exist. Therefore the destruction of all heretics and anyone who deviated from the teachings of the holy church became company policy. The church believed itself to be pure and innocent and so it had to invent a powerful enemy that was leading its flock astray, something that was responsible for all the evil in the world and believe it or not, the Devil or Anti Christ was born.

By the medieval churches standards any god worshiped by the Pagans was considered evil and so they had a wide choice of threatening and frightening figures to choose from as a prototype. They chose an ancient Phoenician deity called Beelzebub or Baal, but he was nowhere near frightening enough to become the personification of evil, so they furnished him with all the trappings necessary i.e. a tail, horns, red skin, cloven hoofs and of course evil smells. Over a period of time the Devil's image was likened to the Horned God of the Hunt associated with Paganism, basically because it fitted in with the general picture that the church fathers were trying to paint. The church had thus created a living Devil, an Anti Christ and it then went on to create a succession of little monsters to cover all contingencies. The church called them Demons, a Greek word for the spirit of an inanimate object. In Eastern religions Demons were demi-gods occupying the regions between Heaven and Earth. Demons were invented by the church and were all little devils who misled mere mortals into having thoughts that were not in line with the teachings of the church. If folk had psychic experiences, it was a Demon occupying their

A Demon whisperer.

mind. If they heard voices it was a Demon whispering in their ear.

Many of the Wiccans in the local villages clung to the old faith 'Paganism', therefore it had to be destroyed. Wicca Craft was re-branded Witch Craft. Witch craft was termed evil just because it could not co-exist with the conventional church. Thus began hundreds of years of persecution and accusation linking witchcraft with the Devil. Until the fifteenth century witchcraft had just about been tolerated by the church. Pope Innocent VIII changed all that when he issued the Bill of 1484 when he urged the clergy to assist in a new mission, to combat the *'heretical depravities'* of witches.

Thousands of heretics throughout Europe were burnt to death during the Church's inquisition.

The floodgates were opened and the burnings and hangings began!

"Every woman with a wrinkled face, a furrowed brow, a hairy lip, a gobber tooth...a skull cap on her head...a dog or cat by her side, is not only suspected but pronounced a witch".

Two of the church's witch finders.

Satan, the Prince of Darkness, was the title given to the Devil by the medieval church and the witch was his friend. What followed was a long and incredible parade of human folly, cruelty and perversion of justice and of course death. It was quite enough to be denounced as a follower of the old religion, to be imprisoned and then tortured to gain a confession. At first they just told the truth about the old religion and its traditions but that was not sufficient, it did not fit in with what their persecutors wanted to hear. The story they were looking for was that of an involvement with the Devil and his army of Demons and a confession of treason against the Church and the state. Once the world was swarming with heretics, now it seemed to be full of witches. During two and a half centuries, witch fever was commonplace throughout all of Europe, nowhere more so than in Germany where more than 100,000 supposed witches were burnt at the stake. There was even a guide available for witch finders called 'Malleus Maleficarem' or 'Hammer of Witches' setting out the guidelines for interrogation techniques. The authors were two Dominican Friars, Kramer and Sprenger, who were both ruthless witch finders.

MALLEVS
MALEFICARVM,
MALEFICAS ET EARVM
hæresim frameâ conterens,
EX VARIIS AVCTORIBVS COMPILATVS,
& in quatuor Tomos iustè distributus,

QVORVM DVO PRIORES VANAS DÆMONVM versutias, præstigiosas eorum delusiones, superstitiosas Strigimagarum cæremonias, horrendos etiam cum illis congressus; exactam denique tam pestiferæ sectæ disquisitionem, & punitionem complectuntur. Tertius praxim Exorcistarum ad Dæmonum, & Strigimagarum maleficia de Christi fidelibus pellenda; Quartus verò Artem Doctrinalem, Benedictionalem, & Exorcismalem continent.

TOMVS PRIMVS.

Indices Auctorum, capitum, rerúmque non desunt.

Editio nouissima, infinitis penè mendis expurgata; cuique accessit Fuga Dæmonum & Complementum artis exorcisticæ.

Vir siue mulier, in quibus Pythonicus, vel diuinationis fuerit spiritus, morte moriatur Leuitici cap. 10.

LVGDVNI,
Sumptibus CLAVDII BOVRGEAT, sub signo Mercurij Galli.
M. DC. LXIX.

Handbook for witch hunters published in 1486 by Dominican Priests Kramer and Sprenger. This work opened the flood gates for the persecution of alleged witches and heretics. It made effective the biblical command of Exodus XXII.18: **'Thou Shalt not suffer a witch to live.'**

England hit an all time low in 1563 when Elizabeth I passed a new statute ordering the death penalty for witches, sorcerers and enchanters. Previously they would only have received a prison sentence. The suspected witches were now to be charged under civil law instead of ecclesiastical law, which meant they would be hanged rather than burned if found guilty. After this time no more witches were burnt in England but this rule did not apply over the border in Scotland.

Witches were hanged in England and burnt in Scotland.

When King James V1 of Scotland became James I of England, a new wave of persecution against all those who practiced witchcraft was introduced. James was a strong believer in the craft and thought all those who practised it were evil. In 1604 he persuaded Parliament to revoke Queen Elizabeth's Witchcraft Act for a more severe one making it a capital offence if a victim of a witch was injured in any way. The act was extended to include a number of European notions of witchcraft including a pact with and worship of the Devil. This act remained in force in this country until 1763. How many poor, old unfortunate ladies and some men were tortured, imprisoned and executed, for nothing more than being psychic, owning a cat, or being a faith healer or clinging to the old faith? Just as Catholics did when the Church of England was invented by a spiteful greedy monarch who started the witch hunting again. This time it was not Pagans being persecuted by Catholics but the old folk in the countryside and remote

No heaven for him, only hell fire and damnation.

villages like Pendle and East Anglia, whose only fault was that they were clinging to what they believed was the old faith again. However, this time it was Catholics being tortured and executed by Puritans who invented stories to remove them. These folk were not evil as they did not have any deal with the devil nor could they summon Demons or evil spirits. Due to the terror that they went through, the torture they underwent and the terrible death they met with at the end of a hangman's rope, they may just be a little angry and as a result may still be here haunting, waiting for justice. This all loving God has created a fair amount of torture, death, pain, anguish, war and suffering in his time. He certainly has a lot to answer for. Anyway who says that God is a man?

The Churches main weapon has always been fear. Oh he is a good God Fearing man! Why should we fear God? I thought he was all love and kindness. The church invented all manner of things to terrify medieval man into submission. It invented Hellfire and Damnation, Purgatory, The Devil, The Anti Christ, Demons, Witches, The Seven Deadly Sins, The Ten Commandments and Judgement Day.

In those days death was an every day occurrence with most people being dead by forty and with many of their children pre-deceasing them. They died in battle, or from poor health resulting from an inadequate diet and disease or traumatic death. Dying was not the problem they did not fear death, they feared the afterlife. They believed in the Church

Moses with the Ten Commandments.

Break one of these and you knew full well where you were destined for; Hellfire and damnation. Along with the seven deadly sins and judgement day, these rules helped to keep us under the control and fear of the Church, certainly from medieval times until almost the present day.

and its' teachings. What else had they got in their lives? When that church bell rang on Sunday morning they had to be there, if not you would face not only the wrath of the priest but also the authorities as it was against the law not to attend divine worship.

If you committed a crime, or sinned, spoke out against the Church, broke one of the Ten Commandments, committed one of the Seven Deadly sins you were destined for Hell Fire and Damnation. Burning in Hell! For how long? Oh yes Eternity. That is a long time isn't it? Punishments on Earth were severe, but they were carried even beyond the grave. The idea of justice, reinforced by the Church, called for reparation and retribution for sinners. It was not unusual for a condemned criminal to be refused the last rites. At a time of deep religious belief the death sentence was therefore worsened by the condemned's belief in the certainty of eternal damnation.

Whilst in Ireland I was being taken to Dublin by a taxi driver who asked me the purpose of my visit. "I'm giving a talk on ghosts" I said "Oh they will all laugh at you, we are Catholics over hear" We got talking about my ideas of ghosts and the fear that the Church installed into people. He said "You are right, when I was a kid and we used to go to church we always used to chase each other round the pews. The priest would come into the church and we would hear his booming voice shouting at us telling us we were all sinners. To be honest we always left the church terrified."

A few years ago I was doing a talk at my favourite haunted castle, Chillingham. There were two sisters in the audience who were Catholics. Their grandfather was hanged in Durham Jail on Christmas Eve 1940. He stabbed his wife (their grandma) to death with a pen knife. When they were little girls they always remembered their local priest walking up to their miners cottage, opening the letter box and screaming "you are all sinners and you will all burn in Hell." He did this regularly and they were terrified. As they said to me "what had we done wrong?"

Would you try it on at the pearly gates knowing full well that you would not be admitted, because of your sins?. Would you go straight to Hell? No thanks, I'll stay here and they have. Thousands of tormented, terrified souls have remained here because they dare not move on. They believed the mumbo jumbo that the Church had been drilling into them for centuries. The Church is responsible for many of the ghosts that are still around.

Remember that we are talking of an intelligence, something or someone who was once alive like you and I. If they can choose to stay because they love the pink flock wallpaper in their bedroom I am very sure that they can stay to avoid Purgatory, Judgement Day and the fires of Hell. As I keep saying I cannot provide any proof but there is still in existence today a law that states a taxi driver should carry a bail of hay in his taxi cab to feed the horse. Similarly there is a law still in the statute books that states that if you know of the existence of a ghost in your house you should include on the bottom of your deeds 'complete with incumbent'. In 1999 a case came before Judge Peter Stratton QC in Derby County Court. A family had moved into Lowes Cottage in Upper-Mayfield, Staffordshire and encountered ghostly activity. They fled the cottage and tried to sue the previous owners. Needless to say they lost their case.

King Edward II ghostly screams can be heard up to a mile away from Berkeley Castle.

None of what I am writing about can be proved. I can give you a couple of instances that give street cred to what I am saying. Queen Isabella, 'The She Wolfe Of France,' Daughter of the King Of France and Wife of King Edward II was committing adultery with the Kings friend Roger Mortimer. They over-threw the King and had him horrendously murdered in Berkeley Castle. She had murdered the King of England, God's Anointed on this planet. She knew where she was destined for when she died. Just before her time came she joined a Franciscan Nunnery in Hertford and insisted on being buried dressed as a nun with a veil across her face, Guess why? However her son King Edward III, saw through her plan and knew that she was trying to get into Heaven and had her buried in her wedding dress.

When King John (who was a naughty lad) was exhumed from Worcester Cathedral he was dressed as a Benedictine Monk with a veil across his face. Why would the King of England wish to be buried dressed as a humble monk? What about the trappings of Kinghood? Where was his crown, his orb and sceptre. He thought dressed as a humble Benedictine Monk that he might get through the pearly gates without being noticed.

Remember it was supposed to be the body of Christ that rose up to Heaven. Imagine this scene; I drop dead and I am floating up to Heaven preparing to get my wings fitted. (I do not think that there will be much of a chance after this book) as I approach the pearly gates, I see St. Peter with a clip board, Inscribed on it the words 'THOSE NOT ADMITTED INTO HEAVEN TODAY.'

"Good morning" he says, *"name" "Er, Richard Felix." "Haven't you recently written a blasphemous book about ghosts? Sorry you cannot come in here."* While I'm arguing the toss a frail little Nun floats up. *"Is it ok if I just pop through the Gates?" "Of course it is Sister I'll just get the keys"* and he shouts *"open up lads there is a good Christian nun coming through."* I shout *"hang on a minute do you know who that is? It's Isabella The She Wolfe of France she murdered her husband".* While I'm arguing with him an old

Benedictine Monk floats up and says *"Is it okay if I follow behind that Nun?" "Of course it is father, off you go." "Leave the gates for a minute lads there is a good Christian monk coming through as well."*

They genuinely believed it, they thought they could disguise themselves and get into Heaven.

The Church invented the Seven Deadly Sins, some venial and some mortal. Purgatory was invented as a place for the purification of the soul to be cleansed from venial sin, as no unclean soul was allowed into Heaven. To speed their way through Purgatory rich Christians would pay for Chantry Priests to pray for their departed soul to gain a quick transition into Heaven. They would even pay to build chapels and religious establishments. Indulgences were also sold by bishops to the rich and powerful to lighten the years in purgatory or to gain a quick exit. The Electors of Saxony had two billion years worth of credit against time in purgatory.

This was fine if you were rich, but what about the poor folk. Only recently, the Pope issued a Papal Bull stating that all children not baptised do not have to go to Purgatory anymore. Thanks a bunch! What about all those poor little mites that had to be buried outside the church yard in unconsecrated ground, without a burial service and are still queuing up to get out of Purgatory.

Although Henry VIII abolished indulgences he still tried to get into heaven the Catholic way. Here he is on his death bed

When the Church of England came into being instigated by Henry VIII, Chantry Priests were abolished as were indulgences. Until on his death bed the terrified

Protestant Henry paid for Chantry Priests to pray for his soul, just in case!

With the advent of The Church of England and Calvinism the ghost population of Great Britain grew dramatically. Henry VIII pulled the safety net from under us, doing away with many of the Catholic doctrines, including Confession. There was no more popping into the confession box, three hail Mary's, forgive me Father I have sinned and can I nip back if I do it again. There was no more of that, once you had done it, in the eyes of the Protestant Church you were screwed. No going back, no confession, you <u>will</u> burn in Hell! Hence the fact that most ghost sightings are from Tudor times onwards. The number of ghosts of Monks and Nuns is due to the religious turmoil created by the country turning Protestant, then Catholic and then Protestant again.

There is a phrase that must be remembered when ghost hunting 'Laid to rest.' In the old days we all expected, in fact we almost craved for a decent burial. That is, six foot of English Earth, in consecrated ground, with a proper service,

A phrase to remember when ghost hunting 'Laid to rest' or as the Americans call it, closure.

conducted by a priest or minister of our religion, with a headstone and our loved ones present. Do not forget we did not expect to be disturbed once we were under the earth.

Quite often human bones are found where ghosts have been reported for a number of years and a common theory is that troubled souls haunt the Earth because they were not buried properly. Could denial of the Last Rites create the energy of a troubled ghost, stubbornly waiting for a proper burial? This would have particular relevance to sailors drowned at sea, murder victims, suicides and soldiers and

Watch hut, erected in graveyards for families to shelter in while looking out for grave robbers.

During public dissection bodies of murderers were dissected, their skin was tanned and used to bind books about their trial, their bones boiled, wired, made into skeletons and presented to the local infirmary.

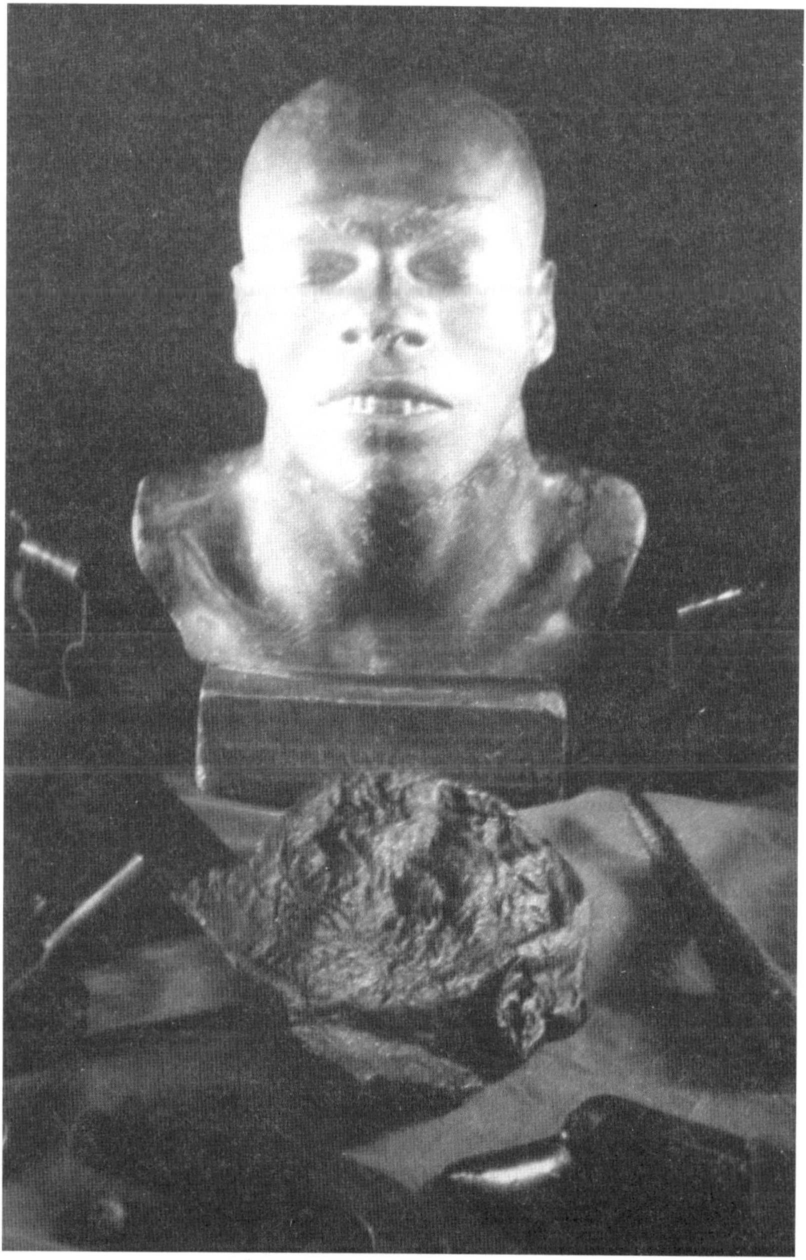

The horrors of dissection! William Corder, hanged and dissected. To the left of the picture a book bound in his skin. Centre front, his pickled scalp with one ear still attached. Behind, his death mask. These items can be seen in Moyses Hall, Bury St. Edmunds

'The sentence of this court is that you will be taken back to the prison from whence you came and from there to a place of lawful execution, where you will be hanged by the neck until you are dead. Your body is then to be hung up between heaven and earth and the fowls of the air to peck at your flesh and the wind to bleach your bones'

airmen whose bodies were never found.

Today we are not so bothered, you can be buried almost anywhere. You can bury the wife in the back garden. You do have to tell someone but I also think that you need a licence to do this.

Even if you got your decent burial in olden days there was every possibility that your body could be dug up by body snatchers known as 'Resurrection Men' (after the rising of Christ from the grave). These bodies were used by doctors for dissection, for the development of medical science. After a funeral, family or friends would take it in turns to sit on the grave with weapons to ward off body snatchers until the body started to de-compose and was therefore no longer suitable for dissection.

If no one was looking after the grave the body snatchers would soon arrive in the dead of night with wooden shovels, a rope, a sack and a little boy. They knew where the head was and dug a 'shute' down to the coffin, which was a narrow tunnel, which would often collapse. The child would be sent down the hole to smash the coffin open and tie the rope around the neck of the corpse. The body snatchers would then haul the body out of the coffin. It was illegal to steal the clothes or the shroud so the body would be stripped, the shroud put back in the coffin, the hole filled in and the corpse taken to the nearest surgeon and sold for dissection for anything up to two guineas. Remember that according to the church we needed to be buried whole, if not, on Judgement Day when the last trumpet was blown, those who did not have a whole body would not have a whole spirit and

The resurrection, the first ghost story.

Only so many executed people were given over to the barber surgeons for dissection until the murder act of 1752 came in. Therefore bodies were always at a premium and body snatchers or resurrection men did a roaring trade selling fresh bodies to doctors and surgeons for anything up to two guineas. This all stopped in the 1830s when the bodies of paupers from the work house were given over for dissection.

would be condemned to Hellfire and eternal damnation. It is only since the Church lost its' grip that cremation has flourished. I believe that there are still only two crematoriums in Southern Ireland. What would have happened if they had cremated Jesus? Well the first ghost story would never have happened. This is why even to this day it is difficult to find enough organ donors.

Murderers and traitors are also candidates whose souls still roam the Earth. You could be hanged for stealing a sheep but could also be hanged for murder. To make the punishment fit the crime the authorities and the church played with the superstitious minds of the condemned. In 1752 the Murder Act was passed stating that 'no murderer was to be buried.' After being sentenced to hanging by the neck until dead, the murderer was then to be either publicly dissected in the Shire Hall or gibbeted i.e. hung up in a metal cage between Heaven and Earth, near the scene of the murder, with the crows eating your flesh and pecking out your eyes, until your decomposing body fell apart. Either way your body was not whole and you did not get a Christian burial and so were destined for Hell.

The same rule of thumb applied to traitors who were either hanged, drawn and quartered or in the case of noblemen and royalty were beheaded. All of these tormented souls were more terrified of what was going to happen to them after death than they were of the actual execution. After beheading King Charles I in 1649 they stitched his head back on before placing him in the coffin, presumably to allow his soul to enter his new Kingdom of Heaven.

When they dug up Oliver Cromwell they took his corpse to Westminster Hall and put it on trial for Regiside (Killing the King). They found his corpse guilty and beheaded it, hopefully sending his soul to Hell, even though he had been dead for years.

Possibly the worst crime in the eyes of the Church was suicide or self murder. They were not allowed to be buried in consecrated ground and were always buried at the cross roads,

Behold the head of a traitor!
Hanging, drawing and quartering, beheading, dissection, gibbeting all meant that the body was not whole and you were destined for hell. The Church is responsible for the lack of organ donors, even to this day!

The grave of Mary Jay buried at the crossroads on Dartmoor. She hanged herself after being made pregnant by the local farmer. A large stone placed on her face and a wooden stake hammered through her heart to keep her tormented soul from rising from the grave.

with a wooden stake hammered through their heart. This is where vampires originate from. The stake was to hold you to the ground as they knew that your tormented soul would not be at rest and you would try to rise from the grave. If you did manage to rise from the grave your spirit would be confused as it would not know which way to go.

Derby Gaol

Although the Church does not really recognise ghosts it has unwittingly created quite a lot of them. Prisons are full of tormented souls that believed that if they moved on from that place they would go straight to Hell.

I saw my ghost at twenty past three on a Friday afternoon. I was alone in Derby Gaol, on the phone talking to a guy from Derby City Council when this grey person shaped figure glided past a cut out window in the kitchen. It was distinctly grey, I could not tell if it was male or female but I sensed it as well as seeing it. I must have viewed it for about four seconds before it went out of view behind a pillar. I then did what everyone does when they first see a ghost converted it into reality and thought someone has just walked in. Although we were not open, so I stuck my head round the pillar and shouted "*Excuse me*" but there was no one there, it had gone. I then went back on the phone and said I may well stay on the phone a little longer than we anticipated. "*Why is that*" he said. "*Because when I put this phone down I will be alone with what ever has just come in and I'm frightened of ghosts*". I did not see it anymore and I have never seen it again, perhaps I will in the future. I believe what I saw was a spirit or soul of one of the many tormented entities that still roam places like Derby Gaol.

Imagine sitting in the condemned cell, on your last night on this Earth, shivering not from the cold but from fear, waiting for daylight and the sound of the Gaoler's footsteps coming to collect you. The terrifying thought of the fate that you know is awaiting you in just a few short hours. You are taken out to the front of the gaol and publicly strangled to death. However, the previous nights terrors were magnified due to the doctrines of the Church, enhanced by the reflections in the book that the prison chaplain had left you to 'digest'. THE WORLD TO COME OR DISCOURSE ON THE GLORY AND TERROR OF THE RESURRECTION.

Books like this were left in the condemned cells to terrify the condemned. Often they were refused The Last Rights by the prison ordinary (priest).

Back to the question at the beginning of this chapter. Why do we not see cave men and youths in baseball caps very often? The cave man died happily without any issues, no fear of divine retribution and Hellfire for him. As for the joint smoking youth with a baseball cap, no fear for him either, no values, no standards, no respect for authority, no God.... no ghost.

'Let the idols that are in them be destroyed
Let holy water be made and sprinkled in the said temples
Let alters be erected and relics placed
If the temples are well built,
It is requisite that they be converted from the worship of devils to the service of the true god.'

Letter written by Pope Gregory concerning the conversion of Anglo-Saxon England to Christianity. AD 601

SCREAMING SKULLS.

"They cut off the heads of enemies slain in battle. Embalm the heads in cedar oil and preserve them carefully in a chest and display them with pride to strangers."

Diodorus Siculus. 1st Century History on Celtic Head Hunting.

Screaming Skulls seem to be peculiar to England, although they may have their origins in Celtic mythology. Human skulls for reasons not known retain some of their original energy which causes them to create supernatural disturbances if they are moved from their favourite house or building. If removed from their final resting place the skulls scream, cause furniture to move and frequently create havoc and bring misfortune to the family concerned.

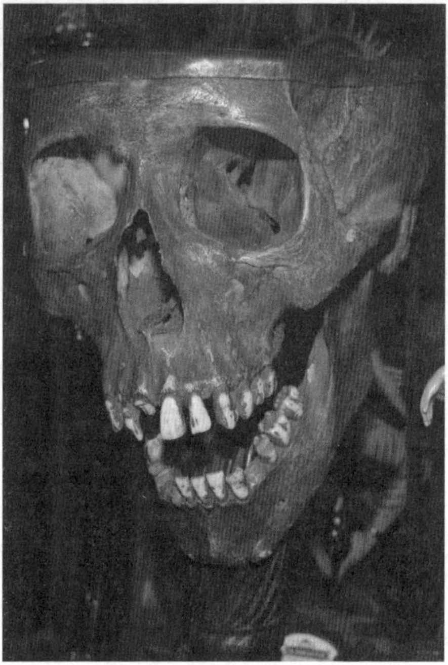

These skulls are found throughout England of which the most famous are:-

Burton Agnes Hall, Yorkshire

Anne Griffiths (Owd Nance) was attacked by two robbers and beaten senseless and died later of her injuries at the hall. Before her death she told her sisters that she would never rest in her grave unless part of her remained in the hall for as long as the building stood. Her sisters were horrified at this request and did not fulfil her wishes. Anne's body was buried whole in the graveyard. A few weeks after her burial her sisters were awoken by banging and slamming of doors in the middle of the night and these disturbances continued for many weeks. The sisters took advice from the local vicar who said that Anne was obviously upset at her dying wishes not being carried out. Her grave was re-opened only to find her body was not intact as her head had been severed and was in an advanced stage of decay. The head was taken into the hall and entombed in the walls and as a result peace returned to Burton Agnes Hall.

Chilton Cantello in Somerset.

The skull of Theophilius Broome has rested in a cupboard in Chilton Cantello Manor for over three hundred years. This was his dying wish that his head should remain in his home for eternity. A lot of his family and heirs were disturbed by this grisly relic residing in the house. Attempts were made over the ensuing years to bury the skull in the grave yard but as soon as this was attempted 'horrid noises, of sad displeasure' were heard throughout the village. These disturbing occurrences only ceased when the skull was returned to its resting place 'the cupboard in the house' and peace and quiet returned to the sleepy picturesque Somerset village.

Wardley Hall, Greater Manchester.

There is a clause in the lease of Wardley Hall which states that the skull of a Catholic priest Ambrose Barlow, executed in 1641 'held there in a niche of a wall on the stair-case shall never be removed.' In similar cases of other screaming skulls disaster is threatened should the skull be removed from the hall.

Warbleton Priory, East Sussex.

This was once an Augustinian Priory which is today a farmhouse. Until the latter part of the 19th century it was the resting place of two male skulls … the owner of the farm who was murdered and his killer who was said to be insane. During building work in Victorian times the skulls were discovered in a recess in one of the walls. Immediately the first skull was buried in the grounds of the farmhouse. However, the following morning it turned up on the door-step. It was brought into the house and placed on a bible where it remained until at a later date one of the tenant farmers tried to take the skull with him when he left the farm. The farmer experienced so many disturbances at his new house that he returned the skull to its original home .

Bettiscombe Manor, Dorset

This story starts at the time of the Monmouth Rebellion of 1685. Two brothers called Azariah and John Pinney were tried by Judge Jeffries, the hanging judge, for high treason. As a result John was executed and Azariah was transported to the West Indies. Later on a descendant of his John Frederick Pinney returned to Bettiscombe in 1800 bringing with him a native West Indian servant who died shortly after his arrival at the Manor. On his death bed the servant pleaded for his body to be returned home so that his spirit would rest. These wishes were not carried out and he was buried in the local church-yard. Soon after Poltergeist activity started at the manor. The family were disturbed by this ghostly activity and as a result had the servants body exhumed and shipped back to the West Indies for burial, minus the head which was retained in the manor house for many years. All was quiet until a tenant threw the grisly relic in the pond and the Poltergeist activity immediately returned. This time so disturbing that the tenant spent a night dredging the pond in search of the skull. The skull was recovered and returned to the manor and guess what? peace and quiet ensued.

Tunstead Farm Derbyshire.

Dickie O Tunsted's skull believed to be the skull of Ned

Dixon a soldier who was severely wounded in battle in 1590. Ned returned to the farm only to be murdered by his cousin who believed him killed in battle and as a result had taken over the farm. It has always been thought that if the skull was to be removed from the farm bad luck would follow. The skull was removed on three different occasions and during the skulls absence a barn roof collapsed, sheep and cows died without reason, and many accidents occurred on the farm. At the same time banging, thuds, and raps could be heard frequently in the farm house. This skull was also thought to be a guardian angel. Whenever an animal was ill three taps would be heard on the kitchen window thus indicating that an animal was ill or in distress. The skull of Dickie also acted as a burglar alarm as it would thud loudly in the night if intruders were around the farm and this actually resulted in the apprehension of a burglar. Dickie's greatest success was when he prevented the London and North Western Railway Company crossing the land belonging to Tunstead Farm. They were constructing a bridge when a series of mysterious land-slides halted the work. Eventually the company decided to divert the rail-way line. The official reason being given was that the landslides were caused by the unstable ground. However, the folks in the area believed differently. Up to present day a bridge on the line has been named after Dickie's skull to commemorate his victory over the railway company. The skull became so famous that post cards were produced in the 1920s.

The George Skull in (Jorrocks) Derby.

In 1992 workmen digging in the cellar of The George Inn uncovered a human skull under the foundations of the building. No screams have been heard but it is thought to cause Poltergeist activity. This skull is featured on every Derby city centre ghost walk and is in residence behind the bar and can be seen by any visitors to the inn. The Poltergeist activity always seems to increase on the infrequent occasions the skull is removed from the building. On rare occasions I take it with me to give a talk or presentation and on my return an incident of

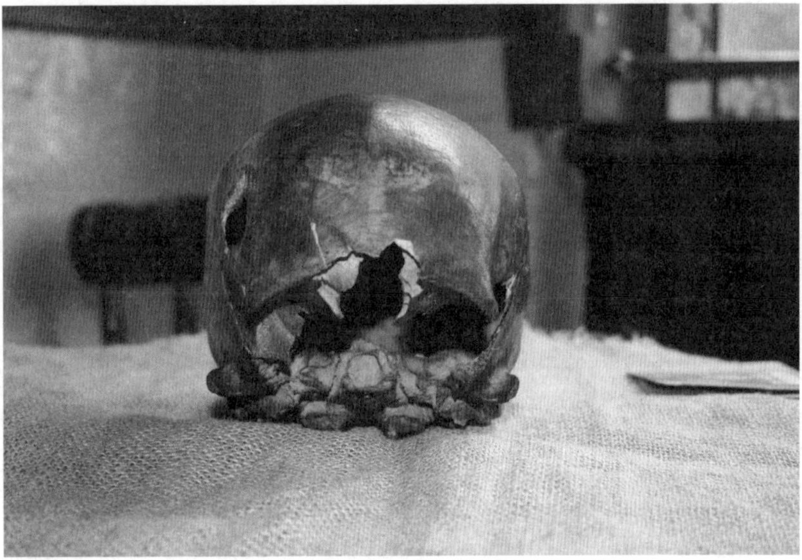

The George Skull., possibly a Viking killed during the battle of Derby 917.

some kind has often happened, such as glasses throwing themselves off shelves and beer pumps mysteriously turning themselves on and off.

These are just a small selection of the screaming skulls that reside in houses and inns around the country… there are many others, but what is it all about ! The skull is only a shell. Do they really still contain some of the energy/intelligence that once dwelt within the most amazing and complicated computer ever created.

Screaming skulls seem to be peculiar to England and said to originate from Celtic mythology. After the slaying of an animal for sport whether it be the shooting of stags, bears or smaller animals it has been tradition to bring home their head or antler and hang them as a trophy on the hunters' walls. The warrior returning from battle would do similar and bring home the head of his enemy and hang it from the tye beams in the home or hang them over a door or window to protect the occupants from evil spirits.

In Celtic times the head was thought to be the centre of emotions and contained a persons' soul and powers of the

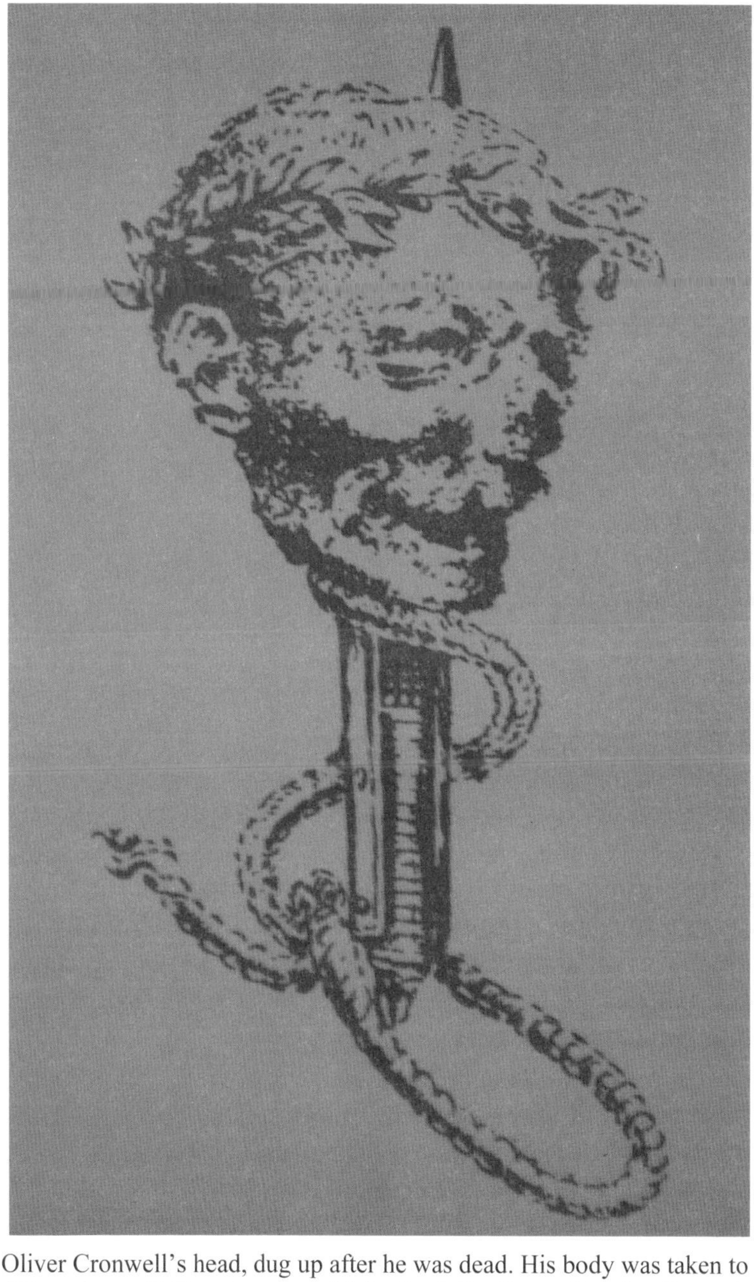

Oliver Cronwell's head, dug up after he was dead. His body was taken to Westminster Hall, and put on trial for Regicide. It was found guilty and beheaded, in the vain hope of still sending his soul to Hell. This skull is still preserved somewhere.

spiritual world. The possession of the severed head of your enemy that you had gained from a fair fight added prestige to a warriors' strength and reputation and made him more of a formidable foe in battle. The heads would frequently be embalmed in cedar oil and stored carefully in a chest and shown to strangers with pride. Sometimes these heads would be impaled onto a fence or gate post as they were believed to start crying and screaming when any enemy was near thus warning the occupants of the house of danger. If a head was from an important adversary it would be placed in a church to which the whole community would offer prayers to it as it was believed to possess magical powers.

Diodorus Siculas in his first century history said of the Celts *'they cut off the heads of enemies slain in battle and attached them to the necks of their horses. The blood-stained spoils they hand over to their attendants and carry off as booty, while striking up a song of victory and they nail up these first fruits upon their houses, just as those who lay low wild animals in certain kinds of hunting. They say that for this head one of their ancestors, or his father, or the man himself refuse the offer of a large sum of money. They say that some of them boast that they refused the weight of the head in gold.'*

In Celtic times water was believed to be a prime source of life. Rivers, springs and wells were thought to be the dwelling place of the ancient Gods. The head hunting pagan Celts believed severed heads to be a symbol of fertility and as a result heads were often thrown into wells in the hope that the water would take on life giving properties.

In 1663 Alasdair Macdonald made a bid for the chieftainship of the Keppoch MacDonalds, and killed two nephews who stood in his way. Two years later Alasdair and six accomplices were arrested and promptly beheaded. To prove that justice had been done the heads were placed in a basket to be carried back to Inverness, but such horrible sounds of grinding jaws and gnashing teeth emerged from the basket that the heads were dipped in the spring to cool off. The place has been known as 'Tobar nan Ceanor' or the 'Well Of The

Heads' ever since.

When houses were built of wood the main supporting beam of the roof was often open to the elements and effected by the wind and rain resulting in damage and rot. To overcome this they hung skulls on these timbers to try and protect them from the elements and to prevent evil from entering the house. When stone replaced wood in the building of houses the skulls were replaced by stone gargoyles.

Even as late as the Jacobite Rebellion severed heads of executed people were set up as decoration above the gates of cities e.g. Temple Bar in London, and Micklegate Bar in York. Still to this day stone balls that adorn our gate posts are a grisly relic of barbaric times.

The remaining skulls that are in place in houses, inns and halls throughout England today are obviously there for a purpose; either because they loved the property or they wished to remain as a spiritual custodian, as in the case of Bran the Blessed who is believed to have brought Christianity to England. Upon his death he requested that his head be severed from his body and be buried where the Tower Of London stands today. He stipulated that his face must point towards the Continent in order to protect England from invasion. All was well until King Arthur had his head exhumed, as he believed that he was not in need of this spiritual protection; perhaps this allowed the Norman Invasion to take place in 1066!

As the skull is a former vessel of human intelligence it might be feasible to assume that they have kept some of the energy emitted by the brain in life. When holding a dowsing crystal in one hand and by placing the other hand onto a skull the crystal starts to move violently backwards and forwards until the hand breaks contact with the skull. The effect on the crystal is immediate and it stops moving in the same way as an electrical appliance stops working when it is unplugged.

England's screaming skulls could well be the last lingering remains of a tradition that holds onto the superstitions that date back to the darkest ages of mankind.

HARBINGERS OF DEATH

"A monk arrayed
In cowl and beads and dusky garb appeared,
Now in the moonlight and now lapsed in shade,
With steps that trod as heavy, yet unheard."
Lord Byron

There appears to be various types of harbingers of death. Many aristocratic families seem to have them, including headless horsemen, phantom drummers, boughs of ancient oak trees that crash to the ground and family members who come back to herald the imminent death of the head of the household.

The Byron family from Newstead Abbey in Nottinhamshire are reputed to have had their own harbinger of death. A monk would always appear before a traumatic event or the death of one of the family. Origins of the monk are not known but their family seat was built on ground that was once an Abbey. Byron actually saw what he called 'The Goblin Friar' before a calamity befell him in 1815 when he entered into a disastrous marriage with the heiress Anne Milbanke. Byron was always fascinated by the supernatural and was indirectly responsible for both Frankenstein and Dracula when he was in Italy with Mary Shelly and his Physician Dr Polydory. He suggested that they each write a ghost story, he wrote a poem, Mary Shelly wrote Frankenstein and Dr Polydory penned the first ever vampire story which later inspired Bram Stoker.

The Welsh have their own Harbingers of Death. The Canhywallan Cyrth or Corpse Candle. These are candle shaped flames that appear near to a house before a death takes place. They say that it is possible to discern from the shape and colour of the Corpse Candle who is about to die. If a child is about to die it will be a small flame, blue in colour. If a middle aged person is to die the flame will be large and red. A large flame, white in colour depicts an old person will die.

The Irish of course have The Banshee which has its' origins deep in Irish mythology. She wailed for many ancient heroes including Brian Boru, Finn Mc Cool and King Connor Mc Nessa. She is a spirit that appears before a person's death to howl a mourning song and to welcome them into the afterlife. It is also Ireland's most famous ghost. The correct pronunciation of this female's spirit is 'bean si.' she is said to associate herself with Irish families – particularly if their surname starts with the letter 'O' – and she is more likely to be seen by a third daughter. Her appearance is said to be the portent of death for a family member, announced by crying and wailing during the hours of darkness. The sound is said to be like that of two cats fighting, only much worse. The tragic relative may be thousands of miles away in another country, and the wailing can apparently be heard for several nights in succession until the actual death occurs. The woman herself appears in contrasting ways. Sometimes she is described as a strange smelling, small, ugly hag dressed in rags. At other times she appears as a young and beautiful woman in a green

dress, her eyes red and swollen from constant crying. A third type of banshee has also been reported, but it is not clear whether she is young or old, as she has no clear features, with holes where her eyes should be. The common factor linking all three types is very long hair that streams out in the wind. Folklore dictates that when a banshee is disturbed by a mortal person she will not appear again whilst that generation lives, but will return to haunt future generations.

In 1922 General Michael Collins was killed in an ambush at Beal-Na – Blath. He was commander of the Irish Free State Army during the Irish Civil War. Just before the ambush the people in the little village of Sams Cross said that they distinctly heard the wailing of the Banshee.

Since the 1840s many Irish families emigrated to America and it is claimed that their Banshees travelled with them. In 1963 a Boston business man with Irish ancestry, who had heard the Banshee before, was on a trip to Canada. He was in bed reading the newspaper when he heard the dreadful noise of the banshee. The time was just before noon on 22nd November 1963. This harbinger of death was bemoaning the death of someone with Irish ancestry, President Kennedy.

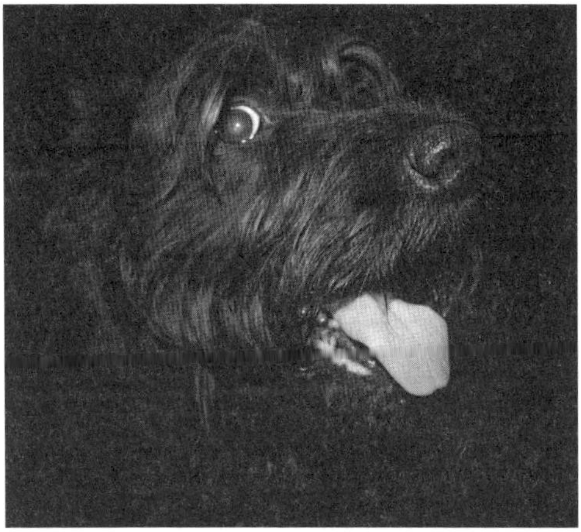

Probably the most famous harbinger of death and peculiar to England and the Isle of Man is 'The black dog.' By tradition almost every wilderness has its' supernatural inhabitant from the Devil, giants, ghosts, fairies, the Wild Hunt, phantom funerals and headless horsemen. In their heyday legends such as these helped to reinforce established values, or to sanction new ones. Early Christian priests often encouraged the legends of men being turned to stone on a Sunday, partly to keep their churches full and partly to discourage people from visiting pagan sites once linked with the old religion.

These legends also had a practical function. Families living in remote parts of the country needed a deterrent to discourage their children from wandering alone onto the moors and hills. Before a police force, wealthy people and land owners needed a deterrent to keep thieves, and poachers at bay. Thieves, poachers, footpads, smugglers and pirates, also needed a deterrent to keep nosey folk and inquisitive kids away from their hordes and contraband. So they filled these lonely places with fearful creatures who roamed the hills and valleys, scratched children to death with their long claws, ate their flesh, drank their blood, and when the foul feast was over, hung their skins out to dry in their caves. Also some ghost stories may have originated from trying to keep folk away, what better way to do this than inventing a ghost.

Fortunately the phantom funeral has gone to its final rest, the Wild Hunt has been banned, the headless horse man rides no more and most folk realise that the devil was manufactured by the Church. However, the black dog is still alive and kicking and is still very much with us. The traditional black dog is larger than life about the size of a calf or donkey, has a shaggy coat, burning red or yellow saucer shaped eyes, and sometimes drags rusty chains. It may be a ghost, a guardian, an omen, a witches familiar or harbinger of death.

Different parts of the country and communities have different names for them. East Anglia has Black Shuck, Yorkshire Padfoot or Bargest, Lancashire Trash or Skriker and The Isle of Man, Moddy Dhoo, Devon has Yeth hounds or Wish hounds. They are mainly encountered in places that were Viking settlements.

Many stories abound about these supposedly mythological hellhounds. Very credible people are still seeing them to this very day.

No less than Fabian Of Scotland Yard encountered a black dog when he was called in to investigate the gruesome murder of a Warwickshire farm worker, Charles Walton who had been impaled on his own pitch fork. Scratched on the chest of the seventy four year old victim was the sign of the cross. While investigating the case Fabian was walking along the main street in Lower Quinton when a large black dog ran across his path. He asked an approaching boy if the dog was his. Frightened to death the lad ran away leaving Detective Superintendant Fabian totally mystified. Later in the investigation Fabian found the body of a large black Labrador hanging from a tree. That night Fabian visited the local pub and got into conversation with some of the locals, on mentioning the dog he was told that back in 1885 a young ploughboy had encountered a larger than life black dog, nine times in as many days. After his last encounter his seemingly healthy sister died. The ploughboy was no less than the murder victim Charles Walton. The strange case of Charles Walton remains unsolved.

A few years ago I was in Skegness for a book signing when a lady came to me with an interesting story of her late husband. They lived in Whitby and he worked at Filingdale. He always travelled to and from work on a motorbike and he often worked late at night. He was travelling home across the moors when he saw what he believed to be a donkey in the road. He slowed down and as he approached realised that it was a large black, shaggy dog with pointed ears and red eyes. He accelerated and left the beast standing in the road. When he arrived home he woke his wife to tell her of what he had seen. They talked long into the night about his experience. The following week her husband was killed by a runaway lorry on a hill in Whitby. She told me she had no objections to me relating this story as long as I did not mention her name. Would you make up a story like that? No, neither would I.

I know a senior lecturer in Psychology, Simon Sherwood, at the centre of Anomalous Psychological Process at University College, Northhampton, who has a Phd in psychology who had an encounter as a child. To quote Simon, *"the year was about 1974. I had been in bed a couple of hours. I awoke to hear a patter of feet. I looked up thinking it was my dog, but to my terror I saw a massive black animal, probably with horns, but perhaps ears, galloping along the landing towards my bedroom. I tried to scream but found it impossible. The creatures eyes were bright yellow and as big as saucers. The animal got to my bedroom door and then vanished as quick as it had appeared".*

Simons parents tried to reassure him by providing him with rational explanations, as most parents do. He was only four years old when he encountered the black dog. To this day he still believes in what he saw that night. He is a rational credible person, a lecturer in Psychology, not at all the sort of person to make up silly ghost stories. He saw what he saw, something that many other folk have seen over the centuries, something that at this moment in time we cannot explain, a devil, a familiar a guardian, an omen a harbinger of death,... lets hope not. I know for a fact that Simon is alive and well and still lecturing in Northampton.

THE POWER OF THE MIND

The human brain has to be classed as the greatest mystery on the planet. If you were to lift off the top of the skull and look down into the brain, you would see something like a walnut with two separate halves. This is the Cerebral Cortex which contains over fourteen thousand million cells. Something remarkable happened to us nearly a million years ago when we seemed to have a brain explosion. The intellectual capacity of our brain increased by over a third giving human kind a huge push up the evolutionary ladder. The brain appears to be in two halves, one mirroring the other. Your personality is contained on the left side and we are still not sure who lives in the right side.

The brain is the best computer the world has ever seen, it is receiver, transmitter, video recorder, video camera, still camera, tape recorder, telephone system and a satellite navigation system. When your computer crashes you have to take it to PC World, whilst ours starts to repair itself. Our brain never tells us 'hard drive full'. Everything we have created and manufactured has been designed by our own computer system. We are amazing. We can be hypnotised and we are all capable of hypnotising others. To quote Colin Wilson in his book 'The Giant Book of the Supernatural,' "*We are unaware that we possess a will beam. We are always allowing it to switch off so we fall into a passive condition.*" We all seem to spend our time in a trans-like state unaware that we are not that far away from Star Wars and being able to use 'The Force.' When Luke Skywalker loses his Light Sabre fighting with Darth Vader he reaches out his hand and the Light Sabre flies back into his hand. We may be capable of doing this as I tried to explain when we dealt with Poltergeists in Chapter eight. Our thoughts have frequencies and frequencies have weight. Light as proved by Einstein, also has weight, which is why space shuttles have light sails.

We have become incredibly lazy over the years. We used to be able to use telepathy but we have designed mobile phones instead. We used to be able to find our way home by dowsing, but we have now invented satellite navigation. We have a small amount of magnetite behind our nose which helps with our sense of direction. Have you noticed how you go into panic mode if your Sat Nav goes down. You never had a problem finding your way before its' invention did you? We are all capable of dowsing. I have taught myself to do it. I can use dowsing crystals, I can use two bent coat hangers and I have

Dowsing with hazel and rowan twigs has been done for thousands of years.

even taught myself to use a forked hazel or rowan twig… the old fashioned way of doing it. I was at Annesley Hall looking for a well, reputed to be haunted by the ghost of a girl, murdered by a local farmer. Her body was thrown down the well and her ghost was often seen by the workers at the Hall. I managed to locate the well although no longer visible and as I stood over it the tension of the hazel twig was so strong that if I had not dropped it I would have broken my thumbs. Three or four days later I started to get terrible pain in my left arm. My wife said it was arthritis or rheumatism which I believed. Ten days later the pain was so bad I went to the doctor and he told me that I had torn a tendon in my wrist. I wonder how? The same also applies to table tilting and glass moving. Over the years I have had some spectacular results. Although I am in no way a 'sensitive' I believe that being a paranormal historian and having researched the haunting I become sensitive to the person and or the place where I am. In other words I often believe that I know who is trying to communicate during the session. Is it the spirit of that dead person moving the table or swinging the pendulum or am I subconsciously doing it. Even this I find paranormal because I am not physically or consciously doing it.

I have the same problem with mediums as I believe we all have the ability to be a medium. I believe that we all have the ability to paint, to compose music and play the piano without being able to read music…. Stevie Wonder certainly can! Hang on a minute, I cannot do it, so he cannot do it, but he can and he can prove it. He just has to lift the lid of the piano and play. The medium cannot do that, he cannot bring your dead grandfather onto the stage to prove it. Therefore we doubt it. "Unless I see it for myself I will not believe it." How many times have I heard that? We used to believe that the world was flat, now we know that it is round, how many of us have been round to check but we still believe it. I genuinely believe that there are mediums out there that are genuine. What does not convince me is. "*I am getting the letter J possibly John or James, can anyone take this*? *I am getting a heart*

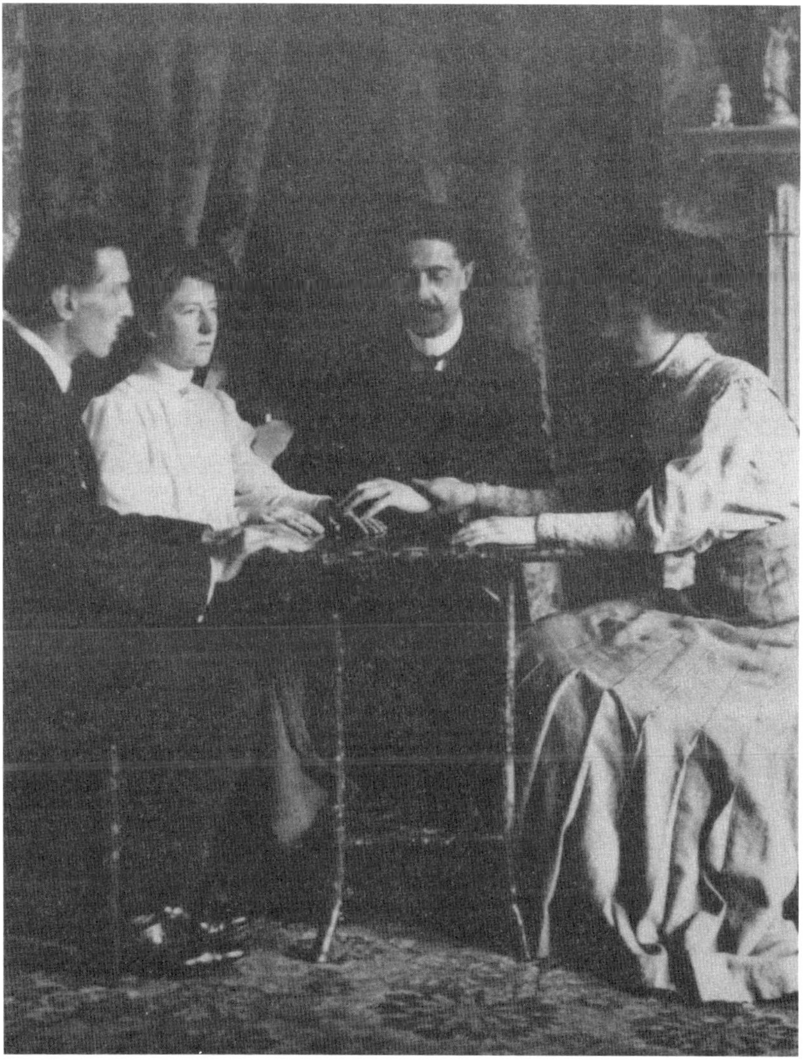

A typical Victorian séance

condition and problems with breathing." Well the heart always stops when we die and strangely enough we stop breathing as well. By the way most men have a scar on their knee.

We all want to believe that there is life after death, but we are all born with a huge negative sign in front of out face and most of us carry it with us for life. Newspapers thrive on bad news just as we do. I bet you are all reading this book looking for mistakes. Yes you have spelt parapsychologist wrong. Oh yes got me, sorry, were the other thirty thousand words all right for you. When visiting mediums we want to believe them, we want to know that mum is ok and so we are on their side before they even start. They can get twenty nine things wrong, two right and we are convinced. We also tend to move the goal post for them. "*I am getting your Dad coming through.*" "*My dad is still alive but my elder brother is dead and he was a father figure to me.*" " *He is telling me he died in a motor bike accident*" "*No he died in a plane crash but he did have a motor bike*".

What I am really not sure about is are they talking to your dead relative, communicating with their soul, spirit or consciousness, or do they have the same ability as the police have, when they have confiscated your laptop. You managed to remove the images that you did not want them to see but they have the technology to retrieve them from the hard drive where they are still stored. The memories of our dead relatives are possibly stored on our hard drive, that are passed down from generation to generation, and a medium has the gift to retrieve it. Surely if that is possible that in its' own right is paranormal.

I am not sure you can actually take a photograph of a ghost. I have seen so many pictures of orbs, I have seen pictures of what people believe to be ghosts or spirits but in my opinion it is a case of "*well look at it, then close one eye,*" "*yeh, yeh I still can't see it,*" "*no, no, no stand on one leg, step back a bit, now turn the picture, there is an eye there, there is a mouth there.*" Beauty is in the eye of the beholder but in my opinion if there is a group of four people standing in this room now and all of a sudden behind me a ghost appears, one of the people see it and the other three do not. The first thing those three say is "no we can't see it." They cannot see it, but that person does, it is in that one persons mind. It is in their perception, they have seen it. The other three have not, the other three are on a different wave length they are all on channel five but the other one is on channel three. They are not tuned in but that person is. How can you take a photograph of what one person sees and the other three do not? Even if that person is taking the photograph. For instance hold up a red flag, everyone agrees it is red, how do they know they are seeing the same colour. What about colour blind people what colour are they seeing possibly green. Is the ghost there at the end of the bed or is it in your head in your perception.

There is a fascinating book, 'The Holographic Universe' by Michael Talbot which states everything we see appears in our mind or perception as a hologram but is in reality a series of waves. He likens it to watching a bowling ball that traces a single line down the lane while you are watching it but every time you blink it becomes a wave pattern.

There is so much more to learn than any of us know at the moment. If you have a vacuum cleaner with a plug which you attach to the electrical socket, it will start to work when you plug it in. As soon as you unplug it the vacuum stops. In three hundred years time when the vacuum has rotted away where is the energy that once powered it. It is still here. We do not have to plug in, we have our own energy source, our own generator. When we die I genuinely believe that our energy source goes on to something else. Einstein told us that energy cannot be destroyed, it can only be changed from one form to another.

Supposedly every one that dies loses twenty one grams of weight. Is that our spirit, soul, consciousness leaving us? After death our brain continues to emit electro magnetic signals for well over twenty four hours. If we are that powerful after death, how powerful are we when we are alive?

I was told a few years ago that the people who are closet to pre-historic man are the Aborigines and Maoris. One of the first things they teach their children to do is dowse to find their way home. You must remember that if a child is two miles away from home looking for water, they cannot jump on a number thirty two bus and ask the driver to drop them off at the top of Brighton Road and then walk down the road to number three i.e. home. They are two miles out in the desert and are lost, the only way they can get home is by dowsing. They teach them by telling the children to close their eyes, walk round and round in a circle and think mum and dad, mum and dad and when they decide to open their eyes to walk in that direction. They follow their instinct, and of course they get home. How on earth do they do that? Have they got a built in satellite navigation? Yes of course they have, we all have. So have homing pigeons, who have Magnetite located behind their beak. Another example is, if you dropped your cat off in Portsmouth on Friday, by the following Monday night it might be back on your doorstep. How? It has built in satellite navigation.

I was recently in Leap Castle talking to Sean Ryan, the owner, and I was telling him this story about Aborigines. He informed me not only that they do dowse to find their way home, but also when an Aborigine dies they all turn up to the funeral. How? Now I don't mean they get on their mobile phones and say *"Hi Fred, Stan died last week" "Ah I'm sorry about that mate, what time is the funeral and where is it?" "Oh its half past three the usual place."* None of that they just turn up for the funeral.

In 1943 Jack Murray Superintendent of the Aboriginal settlement of Delissaville, Darwin was asked to help search for a missing airman. He set off on a motor launch with two Aborigines, one an expert tracker called Mosic. As they went along Mosic pointed to a creek which he insisted they must go down. Eventually Mosic steered the launch towards the bank he said that this was the exact place that was in his dream the night before. As they listened they heard faint cries coming from the bushes. They jumped out of the boat and headed towards the cries. There they found Lieutenant Peter Johnson who had bailed out of his burning plane six days earlier and had been presumed dead. His rescuers had arrived just in the nick of time as he was about to commit suicide tormented by insects eating into his wounds. He was not even the pilot that Murray had been sent to look for. Aborigines believe in Song Lines which are similar to the energy lines running across the

Earth that we call Ley Lines.

I was talking to a science teacher who told me that for many years scientists have been trying to find out more about infrasound emanating from the centre of the Earth. They had recently managed to make a recording of it. It sounds exactly the same as a didgeridoo, the oldest wind instrument on the planet. Where do Aborigines point it when they are playing it? Towards that energy source, towards the centre of the Earth.

I very seldom speak to people that have been frightened when they have seen ghosts. The number of people I speak to that live with ghosts, give them nicknames, just accept them. "Oh George is bumping about upstairs again", it just does not bother them. Most people when they see ghosts have an ability to rationalise what they have seen. Oh fancy dress party is it? Chap dressed in a strange costume. It is only when they vaporize or disappear through the wall that people think 'oh my God I've just seen a ghost' and most people were not frightened. Let me finish with yours and my worst nightmare.

'*Tonight you are alone in the house, its winter, there are no leaves on the trees and it is a full moon. You know that bedroom, the one you never liked. The one that always had an icy chill about it, the one that you always avoided, you always kept the door shut. Well tonight you are sleeping in that room alone. You have a very large ash tree directly outside the bedroom window. The Irish hate ash trees, they are unlucky and would never have one near the house. You come in and guess what, there has been a power cut so you have to light a candle. You dare not go up to that room on your own so you have to go to the drinks cabinet and pour yourself a very stiff whisky. You drink the whisky and all of a sudden you have got some Dutch courage. No such thing as ghosts, not as bad as I thought it was going to be. So off you go along the hallway, up the stairs, very dark of course and the candle is flickering, casting shadows but you are not too bothered and you get to the top of the stairs and then you look down the landing to where the bedroom is. Off you go, you are very tired. You go down to the bottom and you stand by the door and before you even put your hand on the door knob you stop and listen just in case there is anything in there. No sounds at all. You turn the door knob and you fling the door open and thrust the candle into the darkness checking all the dark corners. There is nothing there, how silly. You go in, close the door behind you and get into bed. You leave the candle burning for a little while but you are very tired and you blow out the candle. Before you know it surprisingly enough you are fast asleep. It is then that the wind starts up and starts to blow a gale and it blows the branches of the ash tree to such an extent that eventually the swaying tree causes the branches to rattle on your window. It is a bit like skeletal fingers; rapping on the window. You wake with a start and guess what, shock and horror your worst nightmare is about to unfold, you are not alone in the room. Standing in the corner in the shadows is a dark figure. It has got a cloak and a hood and red staring eyes, black matted hair and fangs. It has got rusty old chains hanging from its skeletal wrists. No point in closing your eyes it knows you are awake. As it starts to glide so slowly across the bedroom floor towards the foot of the bed as its moving its going "oooohhhh" but it gets to the foot of your bed, it stops and it eyeballs you. It looks at you and you look back and it nods its head at you, its coming for you. It starts to bend down and lifts the bed covers and its icy cold skeletal fingers start to reach out up the bed towards your ankles. You draw your feet up as far as possible but no it continues on up until all of a sudden its fingers grasp your ankles and it starts to drag you down out of the bed.'* It is a load of old tosh. It's Grimms Fairytales, it's Monsters Inc. It is what we think ghosts are all about and I swear to you its not.

That was the sort of thing that I was terrified of as a child and I can assure you it has never happened to me and I genuinely do not think that it ever will. Ghosts are not put on

Your worst nightmare.

this Earth to frighten us, I genuinely believe that they are here for a purpose and I believe that often they need our help.

It is believed we only know where about four per cent of the universe is and we believe that we only use a small part of our brain. There are huge areas within it that are uncharted. It is exactly the same as the map makers of medieval times, we do not understand what lies within our mind and therefore '*here there be monsters.*' We have not got a clue what is beyond infinity. If there is a Creator, who created him, and who is to say he is male.... the Church. We do not know much at all about ourselves. There is so much that we do not understand, and we have so much still to learn. Regarding the paranormal we are in the Stone Age. We could be considered to be behaving in the same way as the monkeys who were throwing stones at the Monolith in Stanley Kubrik's film 2001 'A Space Odyssey'.

When I was a kid I remember the coal man coming round with a horse and cart. His horse had blinkers on to stop it from being frightened of passing cars. It could only see what was in front. The blinkers on the coal man's horse have now come off but we still have ours on. We are only looking in front of us. The sooner we take off our blinkers and start to look around us the sooner we will realise that we are the centre of our own universe.

Sir Oliver Lodge made a wonderful statement in 1933 when he wrote in his book , 'My Philosophy' "*The Universe seems to me to be a great reservoir of life and mind. The unseen universe is a great reality. This is the region to which we really belong, and to which we shall one day return*".

I promise you that the reality behind ghosts is far more fascinating than the Scooby Doo side of most ghost programmes, horror films and books. I hope now that you have read this book you will agree with me and have a better understanding of what a ghost could be.

For years I have avoided writing this book because I did not believe that I had all the answers. I still do not. I still have an incomplete jigsaw, it always will be. I started this book saying that eight out of ten ghosts can be explained. That is not quite true, ten out of ten ghosts can be explained but not yet.

I leave you with the thoughts of one of the worlds first

Paranormal investigators Dr Samuel Johnson.

"It is wonderful that six thousand years have now elapsed since the creation of the world, and still it is undecided whether or not there has ever been an instance of the spirit of any person appearing after death. ALL ARGUMENT IS AGAINST IT, BUT ALL BELIEF IS FOR IT"

But those immortal words will live on forever and a day

WHAT IS A GHOST?

GLOSSARY

Amulet an item that has the power to stave off ghosts and evil spirits.

Angel something often mistaken for a ghost, but in fact is a holy and protective messenger shielding us from harm.

Animal ghosts are believed to be the spirits of animals who survive the death process. Many experts in the paranormal acknowledge the existence of animal ghosts and some investigators even believe animals have what is known as a 'collective soul'. This theory supposes that as many as half a dozen animals at one time may share just one soul. Isn't it strange that the only animal ghosts that we see are animals that have co-habit with us for thousands of years such as dogs, cats and horses. Have you ever heard of a haunted abattoir? Or a ghost pig?

Apparitions are recognisable figures that are not only seen, but can be heard or felt. This mysterious image of a disembodied spirit can be recognised as human or animal and even ghostly apparitions of ships, trains, cars and other inanimate objects have been seen. Some are said to appear to warn of a disaster that is about to happen, while others are thought to guard sacred places.

Apport happens when a solid object appears from nowhere, with the assistance of the spirit in the company of a medium.

Astral body is the energy that separates itself from the human form but still maintains the personality and feelings of the individual.

Astral plane can be described as a level of awareness in the celestial world, with its own standards and occupants.

Atmospheric Apparition is a visual imprint of a person that has died, left to be replayed on the atmosphere.

Aura is an energy field that surrounds all living things.

Bi-location describes the phenomenon where someone can be in two places at the same time.

Birds Were at one time believed to be messengers of the dead – when one tapped on a window, it was said to signify that a ghost was looking for another spirit to join in. Certain birds, such as sparrows, larks and storks were said to transport to Earth the souls of people from the Guff, or 'Hall of Souls', in heaven other birds, especially crows, were believed to carry the spirits of humans onto the next plane.

Boggart is a word used chiefly in the North of England to describe a particularly nasty type of ghost. Boggarts are said to enjoy crawling into victim's bedrooms at night and pulling the bedclothes off, slapping, pinching and biting people, especially on the feet. In appearance they are said to be truly frightening, with sharp, long and yellowing teeth.

Bogies like the Irish banshee, are said to make a wailing noise. An unpleasant spirit with a preference for haunting children, the bogie, according to British folklore, is foul-smelling, black, short and hairy with an ugly, grinning face. Perhaps it belongs more to the language of parents, hence the warning: 'Don't be naughty or the bogie man will get you!' Bogies were once thought to be the most powerful of ghosts, having apparently once served the Devil by doing evil deeds against mankind.

Cats next to dogs are the most common form of animal spirits. The ghost cat is believed to have its spooky origin in ancient Egypt were cats were often worshipped, especially at Bubastis, where many thousands of mummified cats have been excavated. Historically the Devil was believed to be able to take the form of a cat, and cats were often thought to be witches' familiars.

Cemetery lights hover over graves after dark as bluish balls of light.

Channelling is a form of spirit possession that occurs with a medium who is communicating with an unseen entity to gain wisdom or gain knowledge of future events.

Clairaudience a skill claimed by many mediums. This is when someone has the ability to hear the voices of ghosts and other sounds that are inaudible to the human ear. These disembodied voices of the dead, or other entities, normally tell of events yet to happen. Many mediums say that they can hear dead relatives passing on information from a place they call 'the spirit world'.

Clairvoyance is being capable of seeing events in the future or past through the mind's eye. In its simplest form clairvoyance is to 'see with sight beyond the normal human range of sight'. A clairvoyant can see visions of events that have already happened, are actually happening or are yet to happen.

Clairsentience is, some believe, a basic human instinct finely attuned and polished. If you are clairsentient, you have the ability to feel and know things that have been, are and are yet to be.

Cold spot is an area in a haunted place where the temperature drops by several degrees. Temperature can also rise by several degrees, indicating the presence of a fire in the past. To appear, move something or make a noise an entity needs energy.

Heat is energy, when the temperature drops dramatically and a ghost appears this means that the energy has been drawn from the room and has been used by the spirit. When the energy has been used up the ghost vaporises or disappears and the temperature returns to normal.

Collective apparition occurs when more than one living person sees a ghost or spirit simultaneously.

Collective unconscious is a term to describe a form of analytical psychology developed by Carl Jung. It represents the collective memory of all humanity's past and is held somewhere inside the unconscious mind.

Conjure is an act go summon a spirit to manifest itself for a desired task or to answer questions.

Corpse candle is a term referring to balls of firelight that can be seen to dance above the ground, sometimes around a house whose occupants are soon to die. The light is said to resemble the shape of a candles flame and accounts of such sightings are prevalent throughout Welsh history.

Crossroad ghosts have been reported for centuries, and no-one knows quite why. Some researchers maintain that crossroads are more likely to be haunted because of the number of suicide victims buried there. The superstition behind interring the dead at such places lies in the Christian belief that the cross is a form of protection from Demons, Vampires and other supernatural night creatures. This theory however, is thrown into doubt when it is considered that excavated human remains pre-dating Christianity have been unearthed near crossroads all over the world.

Deathwatch is a strange turn of phrase connected with a species of beetle known as the deathwatch beetle which taps on wood. Many believe the beetle can sense the approach of death and taps in acknowledgement of spirits arriving to take the soul to its next destination.

Dogs have been reported in ghost form all over the British Isles. These spectral dogs are said to vary in size and some have been described as small but with extremely large eyes. They have been white, black vicious or gentle. The Lancastrians have a ghost dog known at Skriker; in Wales there is Gwyllgi, while Derbyshire boasts Rach Hound and Gabriel's Ghost Hounds, Yorkshire has the Padfoot and East Anglia has Black Shuck.

Doppelganger is a German word to describe a ghost that is the double of a living person. Those who experience seeing their double are said to be heading towards misfortune in the near future. Confusingly, other investigators are adamant that the doppelganger is also an indication of good fortune, though recorded incidences of them being a good omen are rare. People associated with the haunted individual are also reported as having seen the doppelganger at a place where the living counterpart was nowhere near.

Dowsing is the skill of seeking answers and interpreting them through the use of rods or a pendulum. Dowsing is widely used as a simple but effective way of searching for such things as lost coins, water and ghosts. It is also used to conduct geophysical surveys.

Drudes are mature witches or wizards, and reports of this nightmare ghost date from ancient England. The drude is said to be well versed in the art of magic and able to cause a ghost to appear in the dreams and nightmares of their chosen victims.

Duppy is the name given to a well-known West Indian ghost said to be able to walk the earth only between the hours of dusk and cock-crow. The duppy can be summoned from its grave by an act of ceremonial magic to do the bidding of a witch. The ceremony involves mixing blood and rum together with other substances. This concoction is then thrown on the grave of one known to have been an evil person when alive as the duppy is widely believed to be the personification of evil in a human.

Earthlights are balls of lights or variable patches of lights appearing randomly and with no explanation as to what causes them.

Ectoplasm is a strange substance said to extrude from the sweat glands, mouth, nostrils and genitals of some mediums while in a trance-like state. Ectoplasm, or teleplasm, is derived from the Greek works *ektos* and *plasm*, meaning exteriorised substance. There are researchers who claim that the substance is similar to pale white tissue paper, cheesecloth, fine silk strands or egg whites. Others say the substance is like human and animal tissue.

Ectoplasmic mist will usually show up in a photo as a misty white cloud to indicate the presence of a spirit. The mist is not seen when the picture is taken. These mists can vary in colour from grey and black to red and even green.

Elemental spirit is a rather curious type of ghost said to be a spirit that has never existed in human form. For this reason, occultists insist that they are ancient spirits representing Earth, Air, Fire and Water that predate man. Elemental spirits are often associated with haunted stretches of woodland and rivers, mountains and valleys.

Elves are spirits of nature. Spiteful creatures, they are suffering as lost souls trapped between two worlds; not evil enough to go to hell; not quite good enough to be accepted into heaven.

EMF (Electro-Magnetic Field) meter is a device that can pick up electronic and magnetic fields. It can also detect any distortions in the normal electro-magnetic field. It is not a ghost detector.

Entity is a term that refers to an intelligent being that is no longer inside their physical body. They have the power to provide information to all individuals who are sensitive to their vibrations.

ESP (Extra Sensory Perception) represents an ability to gather information beyond the five human senses.

Ether empty space equipped with gravitational and electromagnetic fields (Einstein)

EVP (Electrical voice Phenomenon or Electrical Visual Phenomenon) is a method by which a spirit's voice is detected by means of a recording device. It is also possible to pick up visual mages of a known dead person on computer and TV screens, even when they are not switched on.

Exorcism is a religious ceremony where an

attempt is made to expel a spirit that may have taken up residence inside a house or human being. The ceremony usually involves a clergyman such as a priest, often specially trained, who will say prayers and repeat loud exhortations, often burning candles and sprinkling holy water while incense is burned. Exorcism is actually a modern version of the old Christian practice of excommunication – the rite of 'Bell, Book and Candle' – where sinners were eliminated from further entering the faith by a priest who would ring a small bell and slam the Holy Bible shut, often after reading the Maledicton. The priest would then extinguish the burning candles. Modern mediums claim to be able to conduct exorcisms without the usually religious trappings by psychically contacting the spirit causing the problems and convicting it to move on to the next spiritual plane of existence. In some cases it is believed that ghosts in need of an exorcism are spirits that have not come to terms with their passing, especially where their demise has been untimely or tragic. In my opinion the last thing to try to move a ghost on is exorcism as I believe it is nothing but 'bully boy' tactics on the part of the Church.

Exorcist is an individual – usually a religious holy man – who is skilled in removing demons from within people or locations. In my opinion there is no such things as

Demons, so how can they remove them?

Extras is a word used to describe faces or whole images of people that mysteriously appear on photographs. There are many reported instances of pictures revealing the image of a long-dead relative, or even someone still alive but living thousands of miles away, when they are developed. In the early days of photography, many of these wispy image were faked, but there are a small number of examples that defy explanation today.

Fairies are tiny, invisible mythical beings. The pranks they play are sometimes mistaken for the activities of ghosts or poltergeists. Many types of fairies are believed to exist with each one being connected to an element, as in earth (Gnomes), fire (Salamanders), air (Sylphs) and water (Undines), and the colour green is apparently scared to them. They are said to live in hills, valleys, among the trees and also where there are ancient burial mounds and ancient stone circles.

Family apparition is a ghost that haunts one particular family. When the ghost appears it is an omen that someone in the family is going to die.

Fireball is a Scottish phenomenon. Described as a medium to large sphere, it moves in a smooth and often slow way, most often over stretches of water. Fireballs are thought to be the souls of the departed returning to earth to guide the souls of people who have recently died to the next world.

Galley beggar is an old English ghost referred to as early as 1584 in Reginald Scot's work, *The Discovery of Witchcraft.* This ghost has the appearance of a skeleton and its name is derived from the word 'galley', meaning to frighten or terrify. The classic image is that of a screaming skeleton – head tucked under one arm – encountered on a country road.

Ghost buster is a specialist in clearing an area of ghosts, poltergeists, spirits or other haunted activity.

Ghost catcher is a type of wind chime that will clink together as a ghost whisks by.

Ghost-hunter is a person who seeks to find ghosts or haunted places and tries to determine what type of spirit activity is taking place and why.

Ghost fynder is Richard Felix.

Ghost investigation involves going to an area looking for ghosts or hauntings under controlled conditions. Reports are made to document the events. Listing all the reading of the equipment along with time, weather and temperature as the project unfolds becomes valuable information for the research.

Ghoul is an Arabian ghost which appears in human form. It is a grotesque, evil spirit with a terrifying face that gains its sustenance by robbing a grave to eat the flesh of the recently deceased. The title was also used by T. C. Lethbridge to describe his place memory ghosts.

Graveyard ghost is a ghost believed to have special abilities. According to folklore, the first person to be buried in a church yard was believed to return to guard the site against the Devil. Because this task was so great, a cat or dog was often buried before any human, so it would become the guardian of the dead. I believe that the last place that any self respecting ghost would choose to haunt would be a cold damp graveyard, where only the shell of what it once was lies. The only way that a ghost can haunt a graveyard is if it died there. Sometimes people are murdered in graveyards and during the black death of 1349, one in ten people were in buried alive in graveyards and plague pits.

Green lady are green forms of women that are most commonly sighted in Scotland. A green ghost was what Richard Felix was frightened of as a kid.

Gremlins are a recent phenomenon, originating from World War Two in 1939-1945 when pilots flying dangerous missions reported seeing strange goblin-like creatures in the aircraft with them. A 'gremlin in the works' is a common phrase for when machinery grinds to a halt.

Grey lady is said to originate from Tudor times. Some say it refers to the ghosts of a woman who has been murdered by her lover or one who waits for the return of a loved one. There is another theory that these ghosts come from the Dissolution of the Monasteries, which resulted in the death of many monks and nuns, who would have been dressed in grey habits at the time.

Hallowe'en can be traced back long before the advent of Christianity. Our ancient pagan ancestors celebrated the 'Feast of the Dead' by lighting great bonfires across the country to summon the dead and placate them by offering burnt sacrifices. The Christian Church is said to have moved the bonfire tradition to 5th November, marking Guy Fawkes' fate, in an attempt to dilute the true meaning of the night. Modern witches still celebrate the night of 31st October by holding feasts and performing magic rituals. According to legend, Satan opens the gates of hell at the stroke of midnight and all spirits of evil are set free to wreak havoc on earth. By cock-crow these spirits must return to hell, where the gates are slammed shut at the first sight of dawn. Any spirits left outside would roam the Earth forever.

Haunted chair is an essentially English phenomenon referring to people who have a fondness for a particular armchair coming back as a ghost and being seen in the same chair.

Haunt is the place where the ghost or spirit continues to return. Ghosts usually haunt places and not people.

Haunting is used to describe the repeated display of paranormal activity in a particular area. Some hauntings are thought to be poltergeist energy from a disembodied entity trapped in a certain location or by the energy left behind from a very strong tragic event or accident. Occasionally, hauntings appear to be an intelligent ghost trying to make a connection with someone on the earthly plane to give a message. People can also be haunted, as can any item that may have belonged to someone deceased.

Headless Ghosts are spirits of people whose death occurred because they were beheaded. There is also evidence to suggest that these types of apparitions may be connected to the ancient practice of beheading the corpses of people suspected of being connected in life with witchcraft and sorcery.

Headless horseman in ghost tradition are believed to be the results of riders who may have been ambushed and decapitated while riding at speed through wooded glades. Another theory is that headless riders are ancient chieftains who lost their heads in battle and still wander the earth in search of their dismembered heads.

Incubus descends from European folklore. It is an evil spirit that seduces young women during the night, making them sell their souls to the Devil. Appearing as a ghost like figure it takes the form of a young attractive male.

Iron is believed to be a sure antidote against all kinds of bad magic and evil spirits.

Kelpie is probably one of Scotland's best known ghosts that haunts rivers. A kelpie usually takes the form of a horse that tricks humans into climbing onto its back. It then plunges into the nearest body of water, killing the human.

Kirk – grim haunts old churches, taking the form of a phantom animal. In Denmark the Kirk-grim was said to be the protector of the church.

Lemures is the Roman word given to evil ghosts who return to haunt relatives and friends. Ceremonies to placate these spirits were often held in ancient Rome during the month of May, when they were most prevalent.

Ley lines are invisible lines that run between sacred objects or locations.

Luminous body is the faint glow in a dead body to

signify a soul's impending departure.

Malevolent entities are angry spirits, often seeking revenge. They sometimes attach themselves to a living being, causing them discomfort and distress. They tend to impose their anger or depressed personality on the human being they possess.

Materialisation is the ability claimed by some mediums bring into vision a spirit or ghost. One of the first recorded incidents occurred in America in 1860 and was performed by the Fox sisters, founders of modern day spiritualism.

Medium is someone who can communicate with the dead. During a trance state the medium allows the spirit to take over their body so they can deliver a message to the living, the medium does not remember any of this once they come out of the trance. Today the new mediums refer to this as channelling. The big difference is that nowadays the medium remains completely conscious of what he/she says and experiences through the spirit.

NDE (Near-Death Experience) is when a person dies and is revived after a short period of time. The person remembers their death experience and can recall vision of the afterlife, which include ghosts and other paranormal events. Survivors of this experience say it changes their whole outlook on death and they feel as if they can live better lives after this realisation.

Necromancer is a person considered to be a sorcerer or wizard, who has the power to raise the dead and force the spirits to obtain information about the future.

Orbs are globe-shaped lights of energy caught on film, but only since digital photography was established. It is said that they could be the first manifestation of a spirit. But if this is the case what happened to the second coming? What happens next? Although there are times where they do respond to a command. It is much more likely that they are particles of dust, insects, rain spots or light refraction. This would account for most of them. When you switch on a high powered torch, you will see thousands of orbs or dust particles in the beam, so why don't you pick up all these dust particles on the lens of a camera. Perhaps some of them are an energy source perhaps it is 'tinkerbell', that might be all there is to a spirit.

Omen is a prediction of a future event.

Oracle is a prophet that can communicate with spirits, ghosts and gods to obtain information.

Ouija Board is a board with cards of numbers – zero to nine – the letters of the alphabet and the words 'yes', 'no' and 'goodbye' printed on the surface. A glass beaker or wine glass is placed on the table and the consultation can then begin. The board comes with a planchette (a pointer) and once you lightly place your hand on it the pointer will spell out the answers to the questions asked by the players. Some people believe this game to be dangerous and you could be opening dark doors. I see no difference in standing in a circle holding hands or putting your fingers on a glass and asking 'is there anybody there?'. If you have dark doors to open, then I suggest you do not go and see a scary movie either.

Paranormal is any experience that happens beyond the range of scientific explanations or normal human capabilities, including hauntings, telekinesis, telepathy, clairvoyance or any other rarity that cannot be justified by the five senses.

Perfumed ghosts manifest themselves in the form of a scent. Many people have experiences smelling the favourite scent of a deceased relative, such as an aunt or grandmother.

Phantom coaches are also known as 'death's messenger,' and are apparently seen in silent progress before a death in the family. The horses are always said to be headless and the coaches are described as black and sometimes have the appearance of a hearse. The skeleton-like driver is usually viewed as horrendously ugly, with a fixed grin.

Phouka is one of Irelands more famous ghosts, mostly seen in the form of a horse. Its activity was documented as throwing humans onto its back and taking them for wild rides across the countryside.

Planchotte is a pointer used with an Ouija Board to communicate with spirits, ghosts or entities of a higher plane.

Precognition is the foreknowledge of future events.

Psychic is a person who tunes in to phenomena beyond their five senses and has the ability to see or sense the future, present or past. The talents of a psychic include but are not limited to hearing voices, seeing spirits and knowing what might be happening in the future. Unfortunately these gifts have been misinterpreted as mental illness for some. Psychics have also been referred to as seers or sensitives.

Psychokinesis is the ability to move objects using only the power of the mind.

Psychomancy is the ancient art of reading future events through the appearance of ghosts, interpreting what their manifestations to the living might mean.

Purgatory is the place where the souls of the dead must go to be cleansed of all their sins before being allowed into heaven, according to Catholicism.

Reciprocal apparition is an experience where the individual see and react to one another.

Reincarnation is the belief that once a person dies their soul returns to a new body where it will continue to learn lessons about life and how to reach enlightenment. Many reincarnations may be necessary for the souls to learn and become closer to the goal of perfection. There is no judgement, we only judge ourselves, therefore it is up to us whether we are ready to move on or not. This could account that in past life regression, some people have five past lives, but some have twenty five.

Retrocognition is the foreknowledge of past events.

Revenant describes any being that has returned after being dead for some time. It can describe a ghost, but also creatures such as vampires.

Salt according to ancient customs, is an antidote to all manner of witchcraft and evil spirits. It is said anyone carrying salt in his or her pocket is protected, even against the Devil himself. Placing salt in every corner of rooms in a haunted building is said to subdue wicked spirits.

Scrying is a form of divination in which an individual stares deeply into an object such as a crystal ball, mirror or flame, in order to see an image the might appear. Such images usually generated by a spirit can be symbolic and give answers to a question.

Séance consists of a group of people sitting in a circle holding hands in the hope of contacting the dead. The procedure is conducted by a medium that goes into a trance, as a vehicle for the deceased spirit to take over and communicate with loved ones, sometimes through a spirit guide. Knocking or rapping sounds can also be heard during a séance. The word is of French origin, meaning 'a sitting', there's no limit to the number of participants, though even numbers apparently get better results.

Sensitive refers to a person who can detect paranormal events beyond the range of their five senses.

Shaman is a medicine man or a witch doctor who can communicate with the spirits during a trance and who also possesses the power of healing.

Silky is a female ghost, seen doing domestic chores during the night. They were said to terrorize maids who did not complete their chores.

Sixth sense is to have the power of perception in addition to the five senses. It is also a popular term for ESP. I believe that there can only be an extension of the five that we have.

Smudging is a form of cleansing or clearing a spirit from an area by using incense to purify the area.

Spectre is most commonly used now to describe a ghost that is faked or the result of natural factors that are explainable

Spirit guide is a heavenly spirit or guardian angel that is present and offers help to the individual to which it is attached. This help may be a simple feeling that comes over the person when they need guidance for a problem or situation. Some people claim they can communicate with their guides at all times.

Spiritualism is a belief structure that assumes that spirits and ghosts can communicate with the living.

Spook is a type of ghost found in America that is not harmful. They were supposed to haunt individuals without knowledge of it.

Succubus Descends from European folklore. It is believed to be an evil spirit that seduces young men during the night, making them sell themselves to the Devil. Appearing as a ghost like figure, it takes the form of a young attractive female.

Supernatural is when an unexplained occurrence takes

place out of the realm of the known forces of nature. The experience usually involves spirits.

Table-tipping (typology) is a type of communication with the spirit world by using a table. Participants start out with any sized table and surround it with a number of people. Everyone places all five fingers lightly on the table. Altogether the group chants, 'Table up, Table up'. Usually the table will start to quiver or lift to one side. If someone in the group has strong energy the table might rock back and forth or lift off the floor. At this point a question may be asked with a response from the table tapping, once for 'yes' and twice for 'no'. If there is a non-believer present the table will probably not move. This type of entertainment can be dangerous and is not recommended to those not skilled in psychic science.

Talisman is a protective charm or amulet said to have the ability to ward off evil.

Tash is the Irish word for a ghost, which can either take human or animal form.

Telekinesis is where a person can move an object through the power of thought without physical means to move the object.

Telepathy is a method of communication from mind to mind, sometimes across great distances.

Teleportation happens when an object is transported from one location to another by disappearing then reappearing in a different place.

Time slips occurs when the past and present collide at a location.

Tokolosh is South Africa's most well known spirit. Said to live in rivers, it is seen in the form of a half human figure.

Trance a state between being asleep and awake, is where a medium uses his or her body as a channel for waiting spirits to pass messages through to living relatives and friends.

Transmigration is the belief that a soul can move from body to body through the process of reincarnation.

Vassage is a spirit that inhabits a scrying crystal. During a scrying session, the spirit communicates by forming literal or symbolic images.

Vengeful spirits return from the dead to avenge terrible wrongs that have been done to them.

Vortex is a small tornado-shaped image that shows up on pictures when there is a spirit present. Orbs can apparently be seen rotating inside the shaft. Sometimes the vortex is so dense it can cast a shadow. It is believed that the vortex is a means of travel for spirits in the orb form.

Wakes are a noisy ancient custom of watching over the dead while vast amount of alcohol are consumed. This tradition, especially popular in Ireland, is based on the theory that drinking – as alcohol is a cleanser – helps the spirit of the deceased on its journey to the next world. Music, singing and laughter are encouraged, as it is believed loud noises keep evil spirits at bay.

Warlock is often used to describe a male witch, but this is insulting to many so-called warlocks, as the word has been used in the past to describe a traitor.

Wendigo is a half phantom half beast entity from Canada, which lives in forests and preys upon children.

White ladies have been seen all over the British Isles, traditionally haunting castles, mansions halls and even bridges and stretches of water. They are thought to be the spirits of noblewomen who died or were even murdered.

Will-o'-the-Wisp also known as jack-o-lantern, ignis fatuus, corpse candle and foolish fire is a ball of flame that floats in mid-air above graveyards or marshy areas. These episodes have been recorded since Roman times. The Native Americans believe them to be a fire spirit warning everyone of danger. The Germans thought the balls of flames were lost or trapped souls that could not move on. In

Africa some believed the Will-o'-the-Wisps were witches trying to scare sinners into behaving properly. In Russia, these lights represented the souls of stillborn infants. Throughout Europe when these lights appeared it was thought to be evil spirits that couldn't enter heaven but were not evil enough to be condemned to hell. It would be foolish to follow these strange dancing lights.

Witch is a person particularly a woman who practises witchcraft. Most worship nature, but there are different types. Most modern witches would not use their powers for evil, preferring to help human, animal and spiritual awareness. An unwritten law is that witches cannot reveal to anyone what they are or how they practice their art in the belief that silence is power, and power brings knowledge.

Wizard is someone with remarkable abilities and usually proficient in the art of magic. Most male witches prefer this title.

Wraiths are claimed to be the ghost of a person on the edge of death, whose appearance should be seen as a warning to the witness that their days are numbered. They are an exact likeness of their human counterpart and show themselves to friends and family of the person who is to die.